The Empath's TOOLKIT

A guide to recovery for the overwhelmed empath

ANNA SAYCE

The Empath's Toolkit: A Guide to Recovery for the Overwhelmed Empath
By Anna Sayce

Copyright © 2018 by Anna Sayce
All rights reserved. This book or any portion thereof may not be reproduced or used in any manner whatsoever without the express written permission of the publisher except for the use of brief quotations in a book review.

ISBN: 978-1-7223-6533-2

This book is dedicated to: Alayna & Isabella

Contents

Introduction 1

Chapter One
Empath Tools for Energy Management 23

Chapter Two
How to Heal Overactive Empathy 67

Chapter Two, Part Two
Methods for Reducing Overactive Empathy 85

Chapter Two, Part Three
The Emotional Projection Trap 145

Chapter Three
Making The Most Of Your Empath Gifts 167

Chapter Four
Advanced Energetic Protection for Healers & Intuitives 197

Conclusion 211

Appendix A
Protecting Oneself From Negative Media 215

Appendix B
Avoiding Negative Energies In Public Places 221

Appendix C
Processing Grief 225

Appendix D
Further Reading for Overwhelmed Empaths 233

Appendix E
For Readers Who May Not Have Been Affected By Trauma 237

About the Author 247

**Resources & Further Tools for Developing Your
Empath Skills** 249

INTRODUCTION

How many of the following statements do you relate to?

- You feel the world's suffering on a large scale, and wish you could do something to help
- You know when a person is upset or unhappy, without needing to be told
- You consistently feel the same emotion or physical sensation/pain around a certain person
- From an early age, you have been told you are 'too sensitive'
- You find it difficult to watch the news or distressing images because you feel the pain of the person/people you're watching – as if you were actually them
- You sometimes find it difficult to be fully present to yourself and your own feelings when conversing with other people
- You are prone to feeling overwhelmed in crowds, sporting events or shopping centres
- You often feel shy or self-conscious
- You have a tendency to say yes to the requests and demands of other people – almost as a reflex, without thinking about whether you actually want to or not

- You have a general tendency to put your needs last, or serve others at your own expense
- You have a preference for distance in relationships, and for solitude
- You feel an affinity with the animal kingdom
- You enjoy being in nature, or in places where there are fewer people
- You often feel responsible for how other people feel, and go out of your way to help them to feel better (even when it doesn't serve you). After all, you feel their emotions so keenly!
- You have a habit of letting relationships and friendships get too heavy (and too close) too quickly
- You have a strange tendency to feel aches and pains, but only around certain people
- You have often found yourself in a counselling role in which people dump their emotions on you, and you are left feeling drained by it
- You have noticed that you are a social chameleon, taking on the quirks, behaviours and speech of the people around you
- You experience an emotional over-identification with characters in novels, films and plays. It doesn't matter that they're not real — you can still feel how they felt.
- You have a tendency to forget to have fun and lighten up

- You can walk into a place (for example, a person's house) and get a sense of what has happened there in the past: for example, you either feel positive or negative vibes
- You really dislike watching violent or tragic scenes in TV programmes or movies
- You have often felt that your sensitivity is a curse
- You often know when a person is lying, because the energy behind what a person is saying does not match their words
- People often confide their problems to you (sometimes even complete strangers)

If you identify with at least 12 of the statements above, you are most likely an empath.

What Is An Empath?

An empath is someone who picks up on and absorbs other people's energies – be they spiritual, emotional, or psychological. Empaths can even pick up on energies from places, animals and plants.

What Kind of Empath Are You?

When it comes to picking up on other people's energies, different empaths can 'feel into' various aspects of others' experiences, such as the spiritual, the psychological and the emotional. What a particular empath can pick up on depends on what their particular gifts are.

Below is a list of all of the empath gifts I have come across in my work so far. See how many you resonate with!

Emotional Empathy

Emotional empaths feel and take on other people's emotions as if they were their own. This means that they are able to receive and process other people's emotional data through the heart chakra. This form of empathy can create an emotional rollercoaster for the empath to contend with on a daily basis, as they are often overcome by random emotions, and can get confused about what belongs to them and what does not.

- **Do you know how others are feeling without needing to ask?**
- **Can you feel tension in the air when there's been an argument?**
- **Do you sometimes feel overwhelmed that there are so many people on Earth who are suffering, and wish you could do something about it?**

Spiritual Empathy

Spiritual empaths also pick up on and absorb other people's energies, but rather than processing these energies emotionally through the heart chakra (like emotional empaths do), they process and experience them spiritually through the crown chakra.

Spiritual empaths tend to have active upper chakras, and an expanded understanding of the world and of other people.

INTRODUCTION

Being a spiritual empath gives you the gift of knowing what it is like to be another person, deep down and on the soul level. This gift is activated by looking into another person's eyes.

Spiritual empaths can feel a person's inherent, soul-level urges and values, and know how their soul experiences their human life. It allows them to better understand a person's personality and outlook. In short, spiritual empathy allows us to connect with one another on the soul level.

You may find that you have too much spiritual empathy if you have an unrealistic view of someone, and focus more on a person's spiritual self and potential than their current human behaviors or actions. Spiritual empaths can also sometimes be considered 'pollyannas' or naive by the people around them.

- **Do you have a pattern of getting into relationships based on another person's potential instead of their current reality?**
- **Are you often disappointed when people around you fail to treat you well?**
- **Do you see the beauty and goodness in everyone - including those people that others fail to see any goodness in?**
- **Do you fall in love easily?**

Physical Empathy

A physical empath is a person who can experience someone else's physical state in their body. For example, if someone around you is nervous, as a physical empath you would feel nervous too when you are tuned into them. But perhaps rather than feeling the emotional anxiety (like an emotional empath would), instead you get sweaty palms and begin to take short, shallow breaths, like someone who is very stressed, without knowing why your body is reacting this way.

When massage therapists and body-workers have this gift, they are likely to really notice it while they work with clients. They will be able to feel any aches, pains, or tension in the client's body.

Physical empaths often experience aches and pains (especially headaches) that can come and go while they are around others. They can also experience symptoms of an illness that do not belong to them, leading them to feel like hypochondriacs. What is often happening is that they react to people like sponges, taking on the physical pain of others.

I once heard an interesting story from a woman, Ana, whom I taught in Spain when I was working in a language school as an English teacher. Her father had a serious medical condition which affected his kidneys and bladder, and caused him to regularly pee dark red and black urine. Eventually he died from it, and on the day that he passed away, Ana also urinated black. She was alarmed and got herself checked out medically, but was given the all-clear, and it never happened again. Phenomena such as these are not uncommon among physical empaths.

Another physical empath I know once told me that when a client of hers was describing her experiences with vertigo, the physical empath felt so dizzy she had to excuse herself and go to the bathroom to be sick!

One branch of physical empathy is medical empathy (this is a specialized form of physical empathy). A medical empath is someone who has the skill to diagnose illnesses by means of what they personally experience and feel in the body. Note that medical empathy is not the same as being a medical intuitive. A medical intuitive 'picks up' information about a person and their medical condition, but does not necessarily process the data through their own body, in the way that a medical empath would.

- **Do you feel other people's emotions in your body – for example, getting sweaty palms or palpitations when you come into contact with a nervous person?**
- **Do you 'catch' other people's physical symptoms and ailments when you spend time around them?**
- **Do you often have unexplained headaches or pains when you are around others?**
- **Have you ever felt physically sick when you came into contact with a certain person?**

Psychological Empathy

Psychological empaths are able to gain insight into other people's minds, thoughts, and judgments. They can also join energetically with students or learners – psychological empaths make good teachers because they can see the 'cogs moving in someone's brain.' They are usually interested in thought processes, and how people arrive at certain conclusions. They are also blessed with the ability to see and understand everyone's point of view, and make good mediators.

- **Do you often find it hard to come down on one side of an argument because you can see all sides of it?**
- **Do you understand how people come to the conclusions they do, even when others can't relate?**
- **Are you good at working out what makes people tick?**
- **Have you ever been told that you are good at teaching or explaining complicated ideas or processes?**

Animal Empathy

Animal empaths are those who understand what it is like to be an animal. This gift enables the animal empath to explore the animal's consciousness, including its fears, reactions and emotions. Some animal empaths have a special affinity with one species of animal. Certain animal communicators (i.e. people who can communicate psychically with animals) have this gift. Those who have a collection of pets that others might consider a bit odd or unusual (such as cockroaches, snakes or iguanas) may have an empathic affinity with that particular species.

Animal empaths may be adversely emotionally affected by places where animals are likely to have negative emotions, such as animal shelters, vet clinics, or slaughterhouses.

- **Do you find that you easily form close bonds with animals?**
- **Do you prefer the company of animals to that of humans?**
- **Are you or have you been at some point a vegetarian/vegan due to your love of animals?**
- **When you see a spider or some other unwanted insect in your home, do you make sure to capture and release it outside, rather than kill it?**
- **Do you hate seeing animals in distress, or you feel you have been adversely affected by the energies in places where animals are likely to have negative emotions, such as animal shelters, vet clinics, or slaughterhouses?**

Plant Empathy

Plant empaths are able to join in consciousness with certain plants or trees. Most plant empaths have an affinity with certain types of plant life (it is more rare to have an affinity with all plant species). Plant empaths are able to know what a plant needs, and may dislike being around a plant that is dying.

- **Does it bother you to be around plants that need water?**
- **Are you good at nurturing plants and knowing what they need? Do you have a 'green thumb'?**
- **Have you ever talked to your plants, to encourage them to grow better?**

Environmental Empathy

Environmental empaths can join in consciousness with Mother Nature and the environment. This person may be very affected when ecosystems are damaged, or when trees are cut down and rainforests are destroyed. They are able to move through different landscapes (whether mountains, deserts, bodies of water or forests), and gain a sense of that landscape's power and consciousness. Environmental empaths also tend to feel a sense of trepidation or unease just before a natural disaster such as an earthquake occurs. They sense the changes which occur in the electromagnetic fields of the earth and the sun, and may have emotional or physical reactions to these changes.

- **Do you often feel at one with, or somehow connected to beautiful landscapes when you walk or travel through them?**
- **Can you sense different types of consciousness from different landscapes or energies emitted by the earth?**
- **Do you know or feel 'out of sorts' before a natural disaster occurs?**

Place Empathy

Place empaths can enter a home or a building and feel 'vibes' from the people who have lived there. Perhaps you have been in or visited a house or place that felt 'creepy' or uncomfortable to you. This is because places and buildings absorb energies from those that frequent them.

The residues left behind in places such as hospitals, funeral parlours, cemeteries, police stations, and even historic battlefields may negatively affect place empaths. Place empaths are able to look at a photo of a home or building and get a sense for what it feels like to be inside the building, and the energies that are present there.

Personally I am a strong place empath, and I find that being in Europe, with all its (sometimes bloody) history is an interesting experience for me.

I spent six years living in New Zealand, which has a history of human occupation going back only several hundred years, so the energy there feels relatively clear and fresh. The British Isles, on the other hand, have a history of thousands of years of human occupation, and the energy in some places can feel polluted by old emotional residues.

For example, when I first visited the Highlands of Scotland, I didn't know much about its history. I noticed I was very comfortable in the area around Aviemore, Grantown-on-Spey and the Cairngorms, and not so comfortable in the area around Brora and Sutherland, which felt very sad to me. When I did some research into these areas, I found that Sutherland saw a lot of human tragedy during the Highland Clearances, whereas the area around Grantown-on-Spey has had a more peaceful history. Picking up on these kinds of vibes while travelling is normal for place empaths!

- **Do you get hit with a certain 'feeling' or atmosphere when you walk into a building or home?**
- **Are you able to pick up 'vibes' from possessions or objects?**
- **Do you avoid buying secondhand items or going into thrift/antique stores because the energies in those places or items feel old and stale to you?**
- **Do you sometimes feel strong, unexplained emotions when you travel to a new place or country?**
- **Do you dislike hotels because of all the different energies people leave behind there?**

If you answered 'yes' to two or more of the questions within any of the above categories, you probably have that empath gift. It is not uncommon to have more than one empath gift – the most common ones among my clients are emotional and place empathy.

The Common Issue With Being an Empath

If you are still reading, you've probably established that you're an empath. Being an empath comes with plenty of benefits: empaths can be extremely compassionate, creative, spiritual, and insightful people, to name just a few of their wonderful qualities.

INTRODUCTION

But you may also have noticed that this gift can also cause a variety of common negative side effects. Not all empaths are affected by them - the extent to which you suffer from these side effects will depend on how balanced or overwhelmed you are with your empath abilities.

Some empaths are lucky and remain in balance with their gifts, benefiting from them without suffering the negative side effects. Other empaths fall out of equilibrium over time, however.

This book is geared towards these people; in the following materials we are going to explore how empaths can get back into balance, so that they can use their sensitivity to their own and others' advantage, but without becoming overwhelmed by it.

Are You In Balance With Your Empath Gifts?

Here are some signs you are not in balance with your empathy at the moment, and that you may be suffering what from what I call **'overactive empathy'** - a state where your ordinarily high sensitivity has gone into overdrive.

The Overwhelmed Empath

Note how many of the following statements you agree with:

- You often feel other people's experiences and emotions - experiencing them vividly and profoundly

- You are frequently unable to shake off other people's energies or emotions – these energies actually follow you around, even after the other person has moved on
- You often have a hard time working out whether you're feeling your own energies and emotions, or someone else's
- You have become a hermit and withdrawn socially in order to avoid other people's energies
- You cannot visit crowded places such as shopping centres, stadiums, train stations, or nightclubs because the energies are so overwhelming
- You feel physical aches and pains, or manifest physical signs of nervousness or sickness, around certain people
- When it comes to movies, TV and books, you do not like watching or reading anything that features sad or difficult experiences for the characters
- You often find yourself playing the role of counsellor and caretaker in your relationships and friendships, but you find it a draining role to take on
- You often wish that other people would follow your advice and get their lives back on track
- Your relationships are a source of obligation and stress, either because you self-sacrifice, have a hard time saying 'no' to people, or take it upon yourself to help others with their problems
- You feel like your empath gifts are a curse, and you wish you could be less sensitive.

The Balanced Empath

Here are some signs that you are in balance with your empath gifts - make a note of how many of the following statements you agree with:

- You do not absorb, or feel affected by the majority of the negative energy that crosses your path

- You can walk through a crowded mall without feeling totally overwhelmed. You "mind your own business" energetically speaking, when you're out and about in the world.

- You have learned (or developed) ways to let go of the negative energies you do encounter or inadvertently absorb

- For the most part, you allow your own emotions to pass through you, and most of the time you are able to tell what is your stuff and what is other people's stuff

- You feel other people's pain sometimes, but you do not sacrifice your own needs or over-extend yourself trying to solve other people's problems

- You do not feel the weight of the world's pain on your shoulders, nor do you feel personally responsible for healing it

- You can take in news and current affairs in small doses, without feeling drained or sad in a prolonged way (however, as a sensitive person, you will still sometimes be upset by world events which are indeed upsetting)

- You do not predominantly play the role of the counsellor or the caretaker in your personal relationships
- You don't feel aches and pains (emotional or physical) around certain people
- You can enjoy fictional stories, movies or TV programs even when protagonists are experiencing something difficult (but you still may find gory, traumatic or disturbing scenes to be too much for you)
- You value and honour the gift of your sensitivity - you know that it is an amazing ability that is sorely needed in this world.

Make a note of which of the above statements you identify with, in both categories. Knowing whether or not you are in balance with your empath gifts will help you to get the most out of this book.

Your Results

If you agreed with more statements from section one (the overwhelmed empath) you will benefit from all the chapters in this book – but especially Chapter Two.

If you agreed with more statements from section two (the balanced empath) you will probably find Chapters One and/or Three the most useful.

And if you agreed with an equal number of statements from both sections (overwhelmed and balanced), you may benefit from all chapters.

A Bit About Me

Before we get into the nitty gritty of how you can overcome overactive empathy, I wanted to give you a little bit of background about me, and how I came to write this book.

I was born in the UK in the early 1980s, and grew up in Cheshire with my four brothers and parents.

I have to say that feeling like a misfit, or being 'different' from most people is definitely something I can relate to. I felt it as an empath from childhood (about 8-10% of the world's population are empaths, so we are definitely in the minority)!

In addition, I have always been a very spiritual person, even from an early age, which seemed a bit unusual for a child. I took myself off to church on my own at the age of 11, because this was the only outlet I had for my spiritual side at the time. And although my studies were focused on foreign languages, my weekends as a child were spent reading all I could in the areas of intuition, psychology, the paranormal, and other esoteric topics.

I studied French and Spanish at the University of Oxford, UK, and when I graduated, I moved overseas to work as a languages teacher. However, in 2007, my lifelong interest in metaphysics came full circle, and I felt the call to leave my job working as a language teacher in Spain and set up my own business as a professional intuitive and energy healer. Over the course of the next ten years, I would work with thousands of empaths on their healing and intuitive development.

Empaths tend to be spiritual people, and for this reason there were a great deal of them in my client base. Empaths often already have an awareness of energy, because they have usually realized that they are good at picking up on it from other people. Also, they frequently have paranormal experiences which are linked to being an empath, such as knowing how someone is feeling even if that person is physically located thousands of miles away. Thus empaths tended to be very open to the sort of work that I do.

As a result of this, I was lucky enough to have the opportunity to work with many empaths during that period, and I noticed that most of them felt overwhelmed and overburdened with their gifts, experiencing many of the symptoms I listed above.

The funny thing was that, as an empath, I was suffering from the same affliction of overactive empathy. And the longer I worked as a professional intuitive, the more energetically overwhelmed I felt. I remember really struggling with my oversensitivity in the period around 2008. I wanted to withdraw from the rest of the world, and found myself turning down social invitations, crying over the news, and generally feeling other people's suffering way too much.

I knew that this was not how I wanted my life to be, so I put out a request for help from the Universe, and my prayer really was answered. For the next several years, I went on a journey which helped me to bring my empath gifts back into balance. However, rather than actively looking for solutions to this problem, I found that the solutions were appearing right under my nose, in the form of major life changes that were happening TO me, and which appeared to have the effect of reining in my energetic sensitivity.

I was also lucky in that I was able to channel information on how to solve this issue in my readings with clients. Many of my empath clients would ask their guides how they could resolve their overactive empathy, and the tips and pointers that the guides passed on proved to be very helpful for both of us.

I began to apply these pointers to my own life, and passed them on to other people, many of whom found the information very helpful and even life-changing.

Eventually I began thinking about writing a book about overactive empathy, in order to get this information out there. It took several years for these insights and observations to come together into a plan of action that has helped many of my empath clients to overcome their overactive empathy.

The Empath's Toolkit

In this book, I am going to give you this plan, which is the 'Empath's Toolkit.'

I am proud to say that I believe this is the first plan for empaths that really cuts to the heart of the issues that affect many empaths. I am not going to give you an energetic shielding exercise and then ask you to pretend you are a non-empath ('faking it till you make it').

Instead we are going to go deeper than that – we'll get to the root issues of overactive empathy. We're going to talk about some heavy topics, including how your relationships, and past experiences have shaped you as an empath, and how they are the key to coming back into balance. We're also going to look at the role of past lives, and psychological/emotional projections.

I am happy to say that today I no longer suffer from overactive empathy. Not only that, but I am using my empath gifts in a helpful way, and many of my clients have achieved similar results.

So this book is not just designed to help you to overcome overactive empathy, but also to show you how to thrive as an empathic person. It will show you how to integrate your empath gifts into your life in a positive way, and I will talk about the special role that I believe empaths are here to play in this world.

Key Points from this Section:

- An empath is someone who picks up on and absorbs other people's energies
- The type of energies (e.g. emotional/psychological/spiritual) you pick up on and absorb as an empath will depend on your gifts – there are 8 types of empath gifts
- Being an empath comes with plenty of benefits, but it can also cause a variety of negative side effects

- The extent to which you suffer from these side effects will depend on how balanced or overwhelmed you are with your empath gifts
- This book has been written primarily for those overwhelmed empaths who feel that they are being adversely affected by the energies they are picking up on and absorbing.

How This Book Is Structured

In Chapter One (Empath Tools for Energy Management) I am going to tell you about the five common types of negative energy that empaths most commonly pick up on. I also give you five energy management tools which will help you to quickly and easily shed these energies.

Many empaths have found this chapter enlightening and helpful, regardless of where they are on the balance-overwhelm scale.

Chapter Two (How to Heal Overactive Empathy) **is designed primarily for overwhelmed empaths** – those of you who feel that your overactive empathy is significantly impacting your life for the worse. In this chapter, I am going to go into the root causes of overactive empathy, and how you can work on them to create change for yourself. This is a really meaty chapter, and it can take a while to use and apply all the recommendations offered in it.

Chapter Three (Making the most of Your Empath Gifts) **is for both overwhelmed and balanced empaths**. In this one, we'll look at how you can use your empath gifts more fully in your work, relationships and all life areas, in fact. We'll also cover how you can use your empath gifts to 'read' other people energetically, and gain information about the truth of who another person is.

Chapter Four (Advanced Energetic Protection for Healers & Intuitives) **is designed for overwhelmed empaths who work with clients in the healing or intuitive fields.**

In this chapter, I give you some extra techniques to avoid taking on negative energies from your client in the course of your work with them.

JUST A FEW NOTES BEFORE WE GO ANY FURTHER:

In this book, in examples of people and relationships, I use both the male and female pronouns randomly and interchangeably.

I have also changed the names of my clients to protect their privacy.

In a few places in this book, I talk about channelling guidance from '**Spirit**' - this is a blanket term which refers to the spiritual realm, and includes the Higher self, Spirit Guides, Guardian Angels, Ancestors, in addition to Divine-level energies such as Archangels and Ascended Masters.

Now let's dive into the first chapter. In it, I am going to pass on my tools for empath energy management.

Chapter One

Empath Tools for Energy Management

If you are an overwhelmed empath, you will likely have realized that you seem to be picking up on other people's emotions, thoughts, or even physical symptoms.

But how exactly is this happening?

In this chapter, we'll find out.

How Do Empaths Pick Up On Other People's 'Stuff'?

There are a few different ways that empaths pick up on other people's emotions, and the first is thought to be the 'mirror neuron system.'

The Mirror Neuron System

It turns out that when we see the experiences and emotions of others (such as pain or happiness), it actually activates the parts of our brain that are involved in our own emotions. In this way, other people's pain can become our own pain, and others' happiness, our happiness. And the brain circuitry that allows us to empathize with others in this way is thought to include 'mirror neurons.' A mirror neuron is a type of brain cell that causes us to respond when we see someone else carry out an action as though we have executed that action ourselves.

Almost all human beings have the ability to empathise with others through the mirror neuron system, but it has been theorised that empaths have a extra-responsive mirror neuron system in comparison with the average non-empath. Thus when we see someone hurt themselves, for example, we tend to flinch harder than the average person does.

Electromagnetic Fields

The second way in which empaths are likely to be picking up on other people's emotional energies is through the electromagnetic fields that are generated by the human brain and heart.

According to the HeartMath Institute, these fields emit emotional and psychological data, which can be detected by the extra sensitive among us (i.e. empaths)!

Energy Absorption

So now we have an idea of how empaths are picking up on, and experiencing other people's feelings, thoughts, symptoms, etc.

But how is it that some empaths come away from these experiences feeling like they have absorbed and are **carrying** the emotions they have experienced?

In my intuitive work, I have found that when I tune into empaths' auric fields, they tend to be carrying certain types of energies that non-empaths do not. I have come to the conclusion that when an empath's mirror neuron system fires with more intensity than the non-empath, such that she feels other people's emotional experiences so deeply - **as if they were her own** - these experiences tend to accumulate in her energy field: they leave an energetic residue, essentially.

At this point I just want to explain a little about the energy field, for those who are new to this concept.

The Human Energy Field

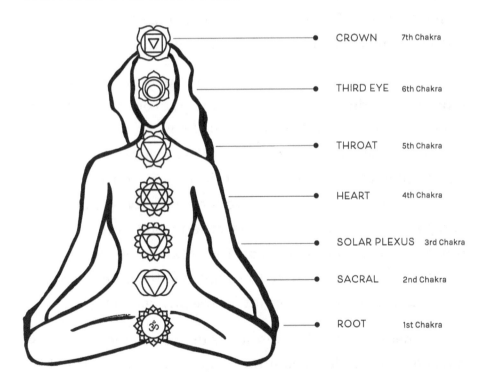

The human energy field - also called the aura - is an invisible field that surrounds each of us.

The energy field encompasses the **subtle bodies** (which are the various layers of energy which make up the energy field). Each subtle body is hooked into the physical body via a chakra, which funnels the energy into the physical body through the meridian system.

The meridians are a set of energetic pathways in the body, through which vital life force energy flows.

The **major and minor chakras** are the main 'hubs' around which your energy is centred. Each chakra receives and assimilates a different type of life force energy from Source, and each one is needed for life here on earth.

The subtle bodies referred to above include the **mental** and **emotional bodies**, which hold the energy of our thoughts and feelings, respectively. Another subtle body that you may have heard of is the **etheric body**. This is the innermost part of the body's energetic field. Because it is so close to the physical body, it is strongly connected to our physicality, and negative energy or disturbances in the etheric body often create problems for our physical body. These two bodies are a close reflection of one another, to the point that the etheric body is often referred to as a blueprint for the physical body.

So the energetic field that surrounds us is a complex, vibrating mass of information about our emotional and spiritual life, our strengths and gifts, physical health, wounds and traumas, and the challenges and lessons that we are here on earth to learn.

Although much of this information can actually be found by tuning in to the seven major chakras, if you are an empath, the energies that you are picking up from other people will mostly end up in your subtle bodies - namely the emotional, mental and etheric bodies.

How This Works In Reality

So let's say that an empath called Emily is watching TV and a commercial comes on which is raising money for starving children in Africa. The images Emily sees cause her to feel the famine victims' distress as if it were her own.

She is triggered. And when this happens, her energy field goes from intact to porous - much like the difference between a bowl and a colander.

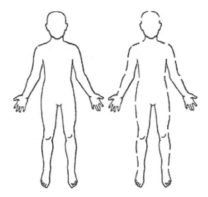

Through her open energy field, she absorbs the emotional data she sees, and it leaves a residue. This is the mechanism by which we as empaths accumulate other people's emotional experiences and energies.

How To Fix It

There is a solution to all of this. We do not want to be carrying around these energies needlessly, and that is what this chapter is all about. I am going to educate you about the five main types of 'energetic clutter' I frequently find in empaths' auric fields, and I am going to give you techniques for clearing these different kinds of energy that you may be absorbing during your daily life as an empath, so that you can feel clearer and lighter.

So what are the five types of energy we often collect as empaths? I have listed them below:

1. Earthbound spirits
2. Unwanted influencing energies
3. Psychic ties
4. Emotional residues
5. Negative thought forms

Next I am going to go into each one in more detail, starting with the first: earthbound spirits.

1. Earthbound Spirits

A very common type of energy for empaths to pick up on is the earthbound spirit. **Earthbound spirits** are the mental and emotional bodies of deceased people who have not fully crossed over after death.

The common feature all earthbound spirits have is that they do not want to cross over to the other side for some reason, and because of this they resonate with negative energies such as 'stuckness,' fearfulness, unhappiness, and pain.

Here are a few reasons why earthbound spirits won't fully cross over:

- Addictions (when a person is dependent upon a physical substance, such as alcohol or some other drug, the emotional and mental body may be so attached to that substance that the person is reluctant to leave the Earth plane upon death)
- Fear of God's judgment
- An extraordinary level of attachment to their loved ones or home
- Lack of awareness of having died
- No belief in the afterlife
- Guilt over having committed suicide
- A need for vengeance
- Any other unfinished business

Earthbound spirits are commonly found in public places that have experienced a lot of sadness and pain, such as hospitals, funeral parlours, cemeteries and police stations. Some may also be drawn to places which serve alcohol, such as bars and clubs.

The Link Between Overactive Empathy and Earthbound Spirits

Earthbound Spirits sometimes attach to people's auras, or to particular locations.

Specifically, they are drawn to the following people:

- People who smoke marijuana (which opens up your energy and attracts earthbound spirits, like moths to a flame)
- Those who get very drunk (so drunk that they lose control and don't know what's going on anymore)
- Those who open themselves up to channel without considering or caring about who or what they might be channelling
- People who feel the emotions of others (i.e. empaths), and who open their energy fields to other people's experiences, often allowing these earthbound spirits into their own energy fields.

Let's have a look at that last point…

Why Earthbound Spirits Are Drawn to Empaths

Many intuitive, empathic and sensitive people have naturally open auras. Empaths are able to merge with other people's energy fields – their energetic openness allows them to leave their own energy body and feel into other people's.

Unfortunately, this energetic openness also causes empaths to unconsciously explore other people's energy fields, and to habitually bring back earthbound spirits with them when they return to their own energy field, without even knowing this has occurred.

If you want to see the opposite of this energetic openness, let's take the example of a 'blockhead.' A 'blockhead' is the silly, tongue-in-cheek name I give to the kind of person you could knock over the head with a plank of wood, and he'd probably never notice.

The 'blockhead' is the polar opposite of the empath. There are some people who quite simply don't notice as much as others - they're what is commonly known as thick-skinned. Their consciousness and point of view is most definitely anchored in their own energy field. They generally don't become 'uncentered.' Often they're simply not as interested in what's going on around them, or in what's going on with other people as empaths are. 'Blockheads' are people who are generally born with closed energy fields.

On the scale of energetic openness, empaths are consistently on one end of the scale, and 'blockheads' are on the other end. If you are empathic, your energy field will be porous and open as you get triggered by other people's emotions, and you may well be attracting earthbound spirits without even knowing it.

Before I teach you how to clear these spirits from your aura and your space, I want to talk a little bit more about why we want to avoid them.

The Negative Effects of Earthbound Spirit Attachment

There are three main reasons why you want to avoid inviting earthbound spirits into your energy field. The first is that they drain energy. One of these spirits will drain a very small amount of energy, but the more attaching spirits you have, the more draining it gets. For example, two hundred earthbound spirits would be a sizeable drain on your energetic resources. Two thousand would be a massive drain on your energy.

To illustrate this point, think of a small electrical appliance in your home, such as an electric alarm clock. One small appliance uses up very little electricity. But if you had two hundred such appliances plugged into your wall, you'd soon notice that you were paying a lot more for your electricity. Two thousand, two hundred or even twenty earthbound spirits are very taxing on the human energy system, in the same way that appliances are taxing on your electricity bill. It's not uncommon to find ten or twenty earthbound spirits following an empath around. Depending on the number of spirits attached, removing them and releasing them into the light can sometimes help to improve a person's energy levels, and make an empath feel more centred in themselves.

Negative Emotions & Earthbound Spirits

The second reason why earthbound spirits are to be avoided is because by their nature they are very unstable, and susceptible to negative emotions. When earthbound spirits attach to a person, they amplify and echo any pain and negative emotion in that person's energy field. So if you feel angry and have one hundred earthbound spirits in your energy field, that anger will be amplified. The same goes for any fear, pain or guilt you are holding. Those negative emotions can certainly be reduced by removing any attaching earthbound spirits, although getting rid of them will do nothing to remove the actual root cause of the negative emotion. Earthbound spirits simply echo negative emotion that is already there – they do not create it.

The third reason you want to avoid earthbound spirits is because they can affect your intuitive accuracy. If you have an earthbound spirit in your aura, you could end up channelling that spirit, perhaps assuming that it's your Spirit Guide.

The earthly equivalent of channelling and consulting an earthbound spirit is like approaching an addict on the street (or indeed anyone with significant problems or issues that keep them very stuck) and asking for advice. As you can probably imagine, the advice is less likely to be helpful or high-vibrational, because it tends to come from a place of 'stuckness' or fear.

Professional Intuitives and Earthbound Spirits

Note that people who do readings for others are also at risk of attracting earthbound spirits, so if this applies to you, please pay attention!

Not only does the professional intuitive have a habitually porous energy field by virtue of being an generally empathic or intuitive person when they're not working, a professional intuitive can also take on earthbound spirits when they ARE working (usually from their clients).

This is because professional intuitives open up their own energy fields on a regular basis in order to do readings for clients. So let's say the professional intuitive is in a session with a client, who has attaching earthbound spirits (which is not uncommon for an empathic and open spiritual seeker). The aura of the professional intuitive is most likely large, open, and full of spiritual light. If the client of the intuitive has attaching spirits, those spirits can unfortunately migrate over to the intuitive's energy field, because it is full of light and positivity. Earthbound spirits will always gravitate towards the aura that is of the highest vibration—the aura with the most light and openness. Just like human beings, earthbound spirits tend to favour people who have the nicest and the most open auras.

An Important Note on 'Negative Entities'

One of the biggest myths about earthbound spirits is that they are somehow negative (indeed, some healing modalities refer to these spirits as 'negative entities'). Earthbound spirits are not inherently negative or demonic. The trait that they all have in common is that they are reluctant to cross over to the other side, perhaps because of addiction, fear, or pain of some kind. This can make them seem negative, but this is a state of mind - not a permanent, soul-level trait. In many ways, they are just like you and me - only not in a body, very stuck and unhappy!

A little further along in this chapter, you will find a process you can use for helping these spirits move into the light, and out of your aura/home. Being able to help earthbound spirits to cross over (and clearing them from your space) is an excellent lifelong skill for any empath to have, and it is a beautiful thing to do - both for the spirits and for you!

Now let's move on to the next type of energy that you can pick up as an empath—unwanted influencing energy.

2. Unwanted Influencing Energy

Unwanted influencing energy is essentially the unseen energetic component of controlling, nagging, bossing and coercing behaviours.

This type of energy comes from people who have an agenda for how you should live your life. It can be sent out about absolutely anything: how you spend your money, your daily routine, which university degree you should choose, how you should dress or what you should look like, how you should raise your children, your political or religious views, and even your sexual orientation.

Note that not all unwanted influencing energies which are broadcast are necessarily received. For an empath to be affected by this type of energy, there usually needs to be a component of nagging or receiving unsolicited advice repeatedly.

The person on the receiving end also needs to be susceptible to unwanted influencing energy, in order for it to be accepted and received. Those who are most susceptible to unwanted influencing energies are those empaths who grew up around controlling, judgemental or overbearing people, or those who now spend a lot of time around such people. If getting the approval of other people really matters to you, or has been really important to you at some point in your past, you may be susceptible to receiving unwanted influencing energy.

Who Sends This Type of Energy Out Into the World?

Unwanted influencing energy doesn't just come from friends, family or acquaintances - it can also come from religious, political, or commercial organisations.

How Does Unwanted Influencing Energy Affect Us?

Unwanted influencing energy can affect us by making it more difficult to recognise our own needs and desires. It can block our intuition and sense of clarity in life. It can also interfere with free will and keep us stuck in our lives, feeling unable to pursue the paths we wish to follow.

A person who is carrying a lot of UIE may feel like he needs to please others or behave in a 'compliant' way - even while he may rationally understand that as a grown adult, this is not appropriate behaviour, and he has more options than he feels he does.

Are You Carrying Unwanted Influencing Energy In Your Energy Field?

Below is a short quiz which can help you to work out whether you might be affected by this type of 'energetic clutter.'

Note how many of the following questions you answer 'yes' to:

1. Do you often feel weighed down by other people's opinions on how you should do things, or what you should choose in your life?
2. Do you sometimes feel like you should be running your decisions and choices (large and small) past someone else before you take action?
3. Do you care a great deal about what other people think of you and your choices?
4. Do you find it hard to know if you are making choices that are truly your own, or choices that someone else (a loved one, or society) has prescribed for you?
5. Is it hard for you to let people know when they are overstepping your boundaries?
6. When you plan to do something that goes against what other people think you 'should' be doing, do you often procrastinate or feel resistance towards taking action?

7. If a problem comes up in such a situation, do you get easily discouraged and feel it's not 'meant to be?'

The more of the questions above that you answered 'yes' to, the more likely it is that you are carrying unwanted influencing energy around with you, which is the energetic consequence of being nagged, bossed, controlled or manipulated.

If that is the case, not to worry – later in this book, I am going to teach you a technique for removing this type of 'energetic clutter' from your energy field.

How to Avoid Taking on Unwanted Influencing Energy

The best way to avoid unwanted influencing energy is to set really clear boundaries with people, especially those who seek to control, boss or nag others. By letting people know when their suggestions and advice are unwanted, we prohibit this energy from entering our energetic fields.

I personally have been affected by unwanted influencing energy throughout my life, as I grew up with controlling parents and grandparents who wanted to make many of my decisions for me.

Empaths do sometimes attract this type of energetic clutter, simply because many of them prefer to avoid conflict as it is so uncomfortable for them. This can lead to situations where the empath unwittingly takes on unwanted influencing energy.

When Advice Is Inappropriate

Most of us dislike receiving unsolicited advice, empaths or not - and for good reason. Inappropriate advice thrust on us can undermine our personal power to identify and fix our own problems. But sometimes it can be tricky to distinguish between helpful, constructive criticism and the type of input that encourages the taking on of unwanted influencing energy.

Here are some things to consider/ask yourself when receiving suggestions from others:

1. **Is this person skilled/qualified to make such a suggestion, and have I explicitly or implicitly asked for their help?**

There are of course some types of advice that are useful because they come from highly qualified people that you have hired to assist you. A good example would be a suggestion from an accountant who you have hired to help you to improve your accounting systems. Or it could be a massage therapist who has some helpful stretches for a tight part of your body.

2. **Does this person often think they know what is best for others?**

Is this someone who is often critical or judgmental of other people and the way they do things? Does this person often feel the need to make others wrong?

****

If you answer 'no' to the first question and 'yes' to the second, this is someone who is likely to be sending out unwanted influencing energy to others (and perhaps you) on a regular basis.

I recently had a session with an empath client of mine, Stephanie, to clear unwanted influencing energy. Stephanie told me that she felt a lot of this energy had come from a friend who wanted to 'make a project' of Stephanie. Stephanie had until that point just ignored her friend's suggestions, which had taken the form of bombarding Stephanie with solutions for a health issue.

After clearing this unwanted influencing energy in our session, Stephanie began to see the importance of speaking up and letting her friend know that her input wasn't helping. She had to do this twice before her friend finally got the message.

Requesting an end to unsolicited advice is the best way to protect oneself from this type of negative energy. Strong boundaries are key.

How to Deflect Unwanted Influencing Energy from Advertisers

Be aware that not all unwanted influencing energy will come from individuals. Advertising and commercial media can contribute to this type of energetic clutter, because it can be in the interests of such sources that you believe you *should* look a certain way, or own something in particular, in order to be acceptable to others. As a result, empaths can also be susceptible to unwanted energy from these sources.

Particularly insidious is the unwanted influencing energy that comes from advertising campaigns targeted towards women, that play on our insecurities and encourage us to feel that we are not enough – not pretty enough, not youthful enough, not successful enough, or just plain not good enough. These influencing energies are often programmed into advertising for cosmetics, wrinkle creams, cosmetic surgery, and weight loss programs.

How can we avoid advertising sources of UIE?

Personally, I avoid adverts on television by putting them on mute. I use an Adblocker when I am surfing online, and I do not read women's magazines.

These are just a few preventative measures that you can take as an empath to preserve your personal power and disallow UIE from entering your auric field. However, if these measures fail (and they sometimes do), there is a clearing process I am going to teach you a little further along in this chapter, which serves to clear out unwanted influencing energy from your energy body.

Now let's go on to the third type of energy that empaths often pick up: psychic ties.

3. Psychic Ties

Psychic ties are small energetic connections that form between you and another person. They look like tiny threads, akin to webs of energy between us. They are created when you interact with someone else, either in person or at a distance. You do not even have to be personally acquainted with someone in order to form psychic ties to them – we can also form ties to people we watch on television, and those we read about in newspapers or magazines.

When these psychic ties form, it means that a minor psychic and telepathic connection has been formed between you and another person. These ties exist on the level of the astral realm and the unconscious mind. This means that you are more likely to think of the other person out of the blue, and be connected with what he/she thinks and feels. Essentially, psychic ties mean you are hooked into another person's emotions or thoughts, in a subtle but impactful way.

You do not even need to feel another person's feelings and have an empathic experience in order to formulate these ties with people. Non-empaths form them too, but the difference is that empaths are usually more aware of and affected by psychic ties than the average person.

Maybe you have had the experience of knowing when someone close to you has just sent you an email, or you have thought of someone and then the next minute, they have rung you on the telephone! These little intuitive messages come through the psychic ties we have to people, and empaths are more susceptible to such experiences.

How Psychic Ties Affect Us

Psychic ties merely constitute a small energy drain when we have many of them (and most of us have lots of psychic ties to people – some of whom we have never even met). If you habitually read gossip magazines or newspapers, you will form psychic ties to those you read about.

Psychic ties do not usually constitute a major problem on the level of our auras, but if we let them accumulate over time, they can clutter up our energy fields, subtly draining us.

Historically, psychic ties have not been a problem for human beings. It is perhaps only in the last century that we have had access to so many stories of real people in the news and in magazines (not to mention on internet blogs and forums). Having energetic access to so many stories and people can be draining on the level of our chakras. The answer is to cut the psychic ties that we form to people, and you can do this for yourself.

I especially recommend that empaths do this on a daily basis, because empaths tend to feel the effects of their accumulated psychic ties with other people more than non-empaths do.

I regularly cut psychic ties to people at the following times:

- Last thing at night before I sleep

- After using the internet. Do you ever feel 'hooked in' to the computer, or as if you have some kind of 'internet hangover' after using a computer? You may have picked up a bunch of psychic ties while you were online, especially if you were on social media websites!
- When I want to disconnect from my work and clear my mind to focus on non work-related matters at the end of the day
- When I'm worried about someone, or feeling preoccupied with an interaction that happened during the day.

Note that it is normal to have psychic ties to close family members and friends, although it is recommended to also cut these psychic ties. Please note that this will not affect your relationship or make you feel disconnected from those you love.

Also note that cutting your psychic ties is not the same as cutting a negative energetic cord.

(A negative cord is an energy structure which exists between two people, containing the negative dynamics and patterns of the relationship. Energy flows back and forth between two people through these cords. Negative cords reflect and contain the challenging or 'shadow' aspects of a relationship, and these energetic connections can be cut. A negative cord only needs to be cut once and when done properly, does not reappear.)

On the other hand, psychic ties are different from cords in that they do get re-established, and need to be cut repeatedly.

Later on in this chapter, I am going to teach you how to cut them for yourself.

Let's have a look at another type of 'energetic clutter' that can affect empaths – emotional residues.

4. Emotional Residues

As empaths, we of course go through life picking up on other people's emotions, both positive and negative. Here are some examples of other people's negative emotional experiences that we come across on a day-to-day basis:

- The emotions of our loved ones who are going through something challenging, such as stress, depression or illness
- The feelings of acquaintances and associates that we come into contact with every day, whose emotional lives we are not necessarily well acquainted with, but whose 'stuff' we may pick up on nevertheless
- Stories we read in the news about dreadful injustices, including acts of abuse and violence.

Because empaths care deeply about other people, they can get triggered by others' pain, and their energy fields open up to the other person. That's when emotions can get lodged in the empath's aura, leaving behind an energetic residue.

How These Residues Affect Empaths

Sometimes the empath will experience these emotional residues as feeling what the other person feels on a continuous basis (i.e. your child feels anxious in the morning, so you also feel anxious all day) or the energy you have taken on may be felt simply as a sense of 'heaviness,' fatigue or negativity that you can't quite put your finger on.

Note that emotional residues can also be found in spaces. A person might live in a home for years, habitually feeling angry, for example, and these emotional residues will become part of the fabric of the building. Public places which see a lot of people coming in and out (such as airports, hotels, and hospitals) also often get filled with other people's negative emotional residues. Place empaths will pick up on (and possibly absorb) these energies.

Fortunately, these emotional residues can be cleared from our auras, and further on in this book I will show you how to do it.

Now let's look at the final type of 'energetic clutter' that empaths can pick up—negative thought forms.

5. Negative Thought Forms

Negative thought forms are the psychological energy equivalent of emotional residues - they are energies created by repeated negative thoughts and words.

Note that not all of the thoughts we think become **thought forms** - the energy of most thoughts actually dissipates once it is spent. But if we (or another person) give negative thoughts enough energy, and they become repeated thoughts, they can take shape as a negative thought form and take up residence, contributing their underlying negative energies to our auras.

Empaths may accumulate negative thought forms if they are surrounded by complainers, gossips, or people with a lot of negative self-talk. Wherever there are negative people, you will generally find negative thought forms. We can also pick up negative thought forms when another person repeatedly tells us something negative about ourselves.

For example, an empath client of mine, Jenny, had an ex-boyfriend who repeatedly told her she was very shy. Jenny is an introvert who likes to spend time alone, but she does not consider herself to be shy. The more her boyfriend mentioned this character trait, the more shy Jenny felt around new people. This was a negative thought form that had been created by him, resonating with the energy of timidity/shyness, and it was something she had taken on. It was even making her feel like she wanted to hide from the world – negative thought forms can be self-fulfilling prophecies!

We don't just pick up these energies from other people – we can also create them, when we repeatedly think negative things about ourselves, for example. Luckily, negative thought forms can be cleared, no matter where they have come from.

Negative Thought Forms & Places

Negative thought forms can also take up residence in buildings. This is a very common type of energetic 'pollution' that can be found wherever there is a history of human occupation. Let's say for example that a few hundred years ago, a wealthy family (who exploit the local workers) build an opulent mansion in their town. A lot of the townspeople resent this family, and when they see the house and walk past it, they think uncharitable thoughts about the owners. Over time, some of these thought forms may attach to and accumulate in the building, polluting the fabric of the place. Thus the location becomes associated with the energies of exploitation and greed, and these energies may affect subsequent owners, as well as how visitors experience the place when they enter the building.

Objects can also take on the negative thought forms of their owners. Second-hand purchases are often filled with negative thought forms. For example, let's say that every Christmas your lovely Aunty Doris knits you a sweater. She thinks you love your knitted sweater collection, but you don't have the heart to tell her wool makes you itch, and that the sweaters she knits are not to your taste. So they get shoved into the back of your wardrobe, and every time you see the sweater collection, you tell yourself that you really need to tell Aunty Doris not to knit you any more sweaters, but you don't know how to do so without offending her.

By the time the sweater collection makes its way to the charity shop or thrift store to find a new owner, it can be filled with negative thought forms. If the new owner is sensitive to energy, he or she will sense the negative thought forms present in the garment, and can be affected by them in a small and subtle way.

Place empaths will tend to be most affected by the kind of negative thought forms which accumulate in land, buildings and objects.

In the next section, I am going to teach you how to clear negative thought forms, along with all the other types of negative energy mentioned above.

Clearing These Five Types of Energetic 'Clutter' from Your Energy Field

In this section, I am going to pass on instructions for clearing each of these types of negative energy from your energy field.

Before you use any of these clearing methods, please make sure you have a good understanding of what you are clearing. It is a good idea to read the descriptions of the different categories of negative energy a few times to allow them to sink into your unconscious mind.

Clearing Earthbound Spirits

Below is a beautiful healing process which helps earthbound spirits to return to the light, while simultaneously clearing your auric field of foreign energies, and helping you to feel lighter.

Here are the steps:

1. First, call in an Ascended Master or an Archangel

Those of you who have experience in the healing arts will know that spiritual healing happens with the help of either an Archangel or an Ascended Master.

Ascended Masters are simply souls who have ascended beyond the need to incarnate here on Earth. They may appear on Earth in human form as healers, prophets, or teachers, but this is not for their own soul growth – instead it is for the benefit of humankind. Over many years, so many people have called on these Masters that it lends them energy, and they become spiritual figureheads that we can call upon for assistance and support.

Archangels are angels of a high rank, much like Ascended Masters – the prefix 'arch' means 'chief' or 'ruling.' My work in the Akashic Records has taught me that there are seven realms of existence in the Universe – each realm holds a particular kind of energy that we associate with life here on earth. And each realm is ruled over by seven archangels respectively. Hence we tend to associate a certain Archangel with a certain type of energy, and we can call on each one for a specific purpose.

Below you will find a list of Archangels and Ascended Masters to choose from - please pick one to work with for this exercise. Note that I have not included every one that I know of - just the ones that seem to be most popular among my clients. Feel free to call on one that is not listed below.

Although these beings are often associated with certain religions, you do not have to be religious to call on them. For example, I am not Catholic, but I enjoy working with Mother Mary, and her energy shows up when I ask!

The Archangels

Below I have named the most popular Archangels that my clients enjoy working with.

Archangel Michael

Archangel Michael is a spiritual protector and warrior - he is often depicted armed with a sword given to him by God. His energy is both fierce and loving. He banishes fear, and reminds us that light is always more powerful than darkness, so call on Archangel Michael if you often feel anxious and need that protective energy in your life.

Archangel Raphael

Archangel Raphael brings the energies of healing, gentleness and love. He helps to soothe broken hearts and heal our wounds. Call on Raphael if your heart feels a bit tender and you need some gentleness.

Ascended Masters

Below you'll also find a few of the Ascended Masters that my students often bring in for this exercise.

Buddha

The name Buddha means 'The Enlightened One' or 'Awakened One.'

Moderation is a key teaching in the Buddhist spiritual tradition – therefore one can evoke Buddha whenever help is needed with balance or finding the 'middle path.' Buddha's energy is helpful in situations or life lessons where moderation is required.

Other energies associated with Buddha include love, respect, dignity and peace. Buddha's presence is a wise and serene energy.

Jesus

Jesus is unconditionally loving, forgiving, gentle, and kind. Because his energy is so unconditional and accepting, it is a very healing energy too.

This is the Ascended Master with whom I am most familiar, having spent many lifetimes in the Christian faith.

Quan Yin

Quan Yin is a Buddhist Goddess. Her name means 'she who hears prayers.' Her energy is characterised by compassion. She represents feminine power and beauty.

Quan Yin also teaches harmlessness (i.e. doing no harm), and has a fierce and protective aspect to her energy.

Mother Mary

Mother Mary is the Ascended Master from the Catholic and Judeo-Christian religions, therefore many Catholics present with this energy around them. Mother Mary also accompanies those whose life purpose is to work with children or help children in some way. Mother Mary helps with all issues relating to children, including fertility, parenting, and adopting, so it is not surprising that parents, and mothers in particular, often present with this energy around them.

Mother Mary is the archetype of the 'ideal mother.' She has kind, nurturing, serene, patient, and loving energy.

Lakshmi

Lakshmi is the goddess of abundance and good fortune in the Buddhist and Hindu traditions. Her energy is found around those who are striving for abundance, including material abundance, emotional fulfilment, and good health.

Merlin

A sage and psychic, Merlin is said to have helped King Arthur during fifth Century Camelot in Wales. Some believe that

Merlin is just a legendary figure and others believe that he actually existed. Either way, Merlin can be called on for assistance.

He represents the inner/subjective realm – internal strength and power, and all forms of intuitive development. For this reason, you may find Merlin around psychics and those who are interested in metaphysical topics. If you are on a path of psychic development, you might like to call on Merlin to help you on your path.

****

So now you have chosen your Archangel/Ascended Master, here is how you call in that being for this clearing:

- Say **Archangel Michael** (or whichever being you have chosen), **please be with me.**
- Do the following breathing exercises: inhale to the count of four, hold to the count of four, and exhale to the count of eight. Do this a total of three times.

Now that you have called in an Ascended Master/Archangel, it is time to prepare your space energetically for the healing:

2. Ask for violet flames and white light for the room you are in. The violet flames are a receptacle for cleared negative energies, and the white light is to protect your space.

   Archangel Michael (or the Divine-level energy you personally called in for this), **I ask that you fill and surround this place with your violet flame, removing and neutralising any**

negative energy, and raising the energy in these places to a high vibration of love.

Thank you.

Please place your white light of protection around this place, so that only high- vibrational energies may enter. Please also place this light of protection around my energy field. Thank you.

I ask for a temple of love, light, healing and transformation to be anchored through me now and I send my root chakra energy to the core of mother Earth, to ground me.

3. Next, say the following prayer:

   I call forth all earthbound spirits attached to my energy field/home/car/workplace, for healing now. This is a ceremony to bring you release from the earth plane, so that you can move on to much a better place.

   Dear souls, you are healed and forgiven (repeat the words "you are healed and forgiven" until you are sleepy, sigh, yawn or until you sense that the spirits have released resistance to crossing over to the other side. This usually takes somewhere between 10 seconds and five minutes).

   Know that your life on earth is over. It is completely finished. It was whatever it was, and it is time to let it go.

   You are completely safe and the presence of the Divine is with you. You are filled with Divine light, to illuminate the way forward to your next right place of expression. You are filled

with Divine Love, as you are beloved by the Creator and worthy of love. You are filled with Divine Truth, as you realise that the earth plane is no longer your home. There is a much better place for you to go to.

You are free from fear, suffering, and any other heavy emotions which have kept you stuck.

Dear souls, it is now time for you to move on to the other side, where your loved ones are waiting for you to join them in Spirit. Archangel Michael will guide you now to your own personal heaven. The energies of love, joy and peace await you there.

I ask Archangel Michael to bring down a stream of golden light to guide each of you back into the light of Spirit now.

4. Cut all psychic ties

    I also call on Archangel Michael (or whichever Archangel or Ascended Master you called on before) **to hereby cut all psychic ties between me and any and all of the earthbound spirits being helped today. Please also cut any psychic ties between these spirits and my home/car/workplace** (or wherever you cleared these spirits from.) **Please dissolve these ties of energy in every dimension with a golden light beam.**

    Now bring in new love, light and peace for everyone concerned. Thank you. It is done, it is done, it is done.

5. Close off your aura

   I call on Archangel Michael to fill and surround me with Divine Love, Divine Truth, and Divine Light. Please close off my energy field to all beings except my Higher Self and those beings of the highest consciousness, who are meant to be with me on my spiritual path.

6. Thank the Ascended Master/Archangel you called in at the beginning:

   I send my thanks to Archangel Michael.

Explanation of the Prayer's Wording

Everything in this prayer is designed to soothe the earthbound spirits and encourage them to cross over. The repetition aspect to the prayer "You are healed and forgiven" is quite important, as the repetition is soothing and helps the spirits to relax, releasing any resistance to crossing over to the other side.

The underlying emotion of the prayer is one of peace and love – through this prayer, the lost spirits are reminded that they are divinely created beings, with another place to be. They are reminded that the Creator loves them. They are reminded of the truth of who they are, and that they do not have to be tied to the earth's vibrations anymore. And finally, they are reminded that they are forgiven for anything they feel they did wrong in their most recent lifetime. Any resistance to crossing over is healed.

How to Avoid Earthbound Spirits Altogether

Next, I want to give you a piece of homework that you can do to reprogram your subconscious mind so that you do not engage with these spirits in the future.

This piece of homework is in the form of a prayer, which goes as follows:

I close off my energy field to all except my Higher Self, and those beings of the highest consciousness, who are meant to be with me on my spiritual path.

I recommend that empaths recite this prayer, over and over, for three minutes a day for a total of 21 days. While you say this prayer, you are reprogramming your subconscious mind, so do ensure that there are no other words that you can hear at the same time (i.e. no television/radio on in the background).

How This Prayer Works

This prayer closes off your energy field to all beings except your Higher Self, Spirit Guides, Guardian Angels, Ancestors, and any other beings that are meant to be with you on your soul's path. This effectively bars 'just any old spirit' from communicating with you, so that you do not need to worry about attracting earthbound spirits in the future.

How Often to Use the Prayer

Once you have reprogrammed your subconscious in this way, I recommend you use the earthbound spirit clearing process to clear your space periodically. I do it for my home about once a month. I also use it to clear hotels or other places I will be staying overnight or spending a lot of time in.

Next, let's look at the prayer for clearing Unwanted Influencing Energies.

CLEARING UNWANTED INFLUENCING ENERGIES:

Here are the steps for doing this:

1. First, call in an Ascended Master or Archangel

   Say **Archangel Michael** (or whichever being you have chosen), **please be with me.**

   Do the following breathing exercises: inhale to the count of four, hold to the count of four, and exhale to the count of eight. Do this a total of three times.

2. Say the following prayer:

   Archangel Michael, please lend your assistance to this process of healing and release of any unwanted energies I am carrying that make it harder for me to know and recognise my own true desires and values.

   Please bring forward any and all of these influencing energies in my energy field/in my home/in everything that I own, from unwanted sources; energy that does not support or align with my authenticity, personal power, peace of mind or prosperity in this world.

Please dissolve it into pure light, so that I can feel free to give myself permission to live my life in the way that I choose; according to my own values, desires and opinions.

Please locate any underlying beliefs or thought forms in me which contribute to any susceptibility I may have to this unwanted influencing energy. Please remove those now and cleanse everything so I am less likely to take this energy on in future.

Please help me to verbalise and set out the necessary boundaries in my life which can help to repel this unwanted influencing energy.

I call upon Archangel Michael to dissolve all psychic ties which exist between me and any sources of unwanted influencing energy that are not in my highest good. Please dissolve these with a beam of gold light, in every dimension, through time and space. Please fill me with new love, truth, light and power. Thank you.

It is done; it is done; it is done.

3. Thank the Ascended Master/Archangel

How Often To Use This Prayer

I recommend using the prayer for removing unwanted influencing energies every couple of months (if you have a lot of controlling or domineering types in your life, you might want to do it more often).

Clearing Psychic Ties

Here is the process you can use for clearing away all of those little thought connections you create on a daily basis. Doing this regularly helps empaths to feel lighter, clearer and more centred.

Here are the steps for doing this:

1. First, call in an Ascended Master/Archangel

   Say: **Archangel Michael** (or whichever Divine energy you have chosen), **please be with me.**

   Do the following breathing exercises: inhale to the count of four, hold to the count of four, and exhale to the count of eight. Do this a total of three times.

2. Say the following prayer:

   Archangel Michael (or whichever Ascended Master/Archangel you called in), **I ask you to bring forward all the psychic ties that may have formed between me and anyone I've engaged with *in the past 24 hours/3 weeks/ since birth (depending on when you last did this).**

   Archangel Michael, please dissolve all of these ties with a beam of golden light, in every dimension, through time and space, to allow for more peace and space in my energy field, and less interference from other peoples' thoughts and energies. Now please fill me with the energies of love, truth, light, peace and power. Thank you.

*If this is the first time you have done this exercise, ask Archangel Michael to clear "all psychic ties that may have formed between me and anyone I've engaged with **since birth**..."

How Often To Use This Prayer

I recommend using this prayer on a daily basis, as you will be forming new psychic ties constantly. I like to do it at the end of the day, before I go to sleep.

Clearing Emotional Energy/Residues

Here are the steps for clearing out emotional energy that does not belong to you:

1. First, call in an Ascended Master/Archangel

    Say: **Archangel Michael** (or whichever Divine energy you have chosen), **please be with me.**

    Do the following breathing exercises: inhale to the count of four, hold to the count of four, and exhale to the count of eight. Do this a total of three times.

    Next say the following prayer:

    Please remove from my energy field any suffering, fear, anxiety, anger, shame, discomfort or any other negative emotional energies that do not belong to me.

    Remove from my aura anything that is not my burden to carry.

    Remove from my aura anything that is not my burden to carry.

Remove from my aura anything that is not my burden to carry.

Cleanse my aura of all this negative emotional energy now.

2. Next, choose energies you would like to be filled with instead, such as strength, peace, or self-love, and say, please fill me with strength, confidence, self-love and self-trust (or whatever it is you wish to be filled with).

3. Thank the Ascended Master/Archangel you brought in for this healing.

How Often To Use This Prayer

I recommend using the prayer for removing emotional residues on a daily basis. This type of energetic clutter is one that empaths pick up frequently and as such, you will need to clear it on a regular basis.

Clearing Negative Thought Forms

Here are the steps for clearing out negative thought forms that do not belong to you:

1. First, call in an Ascended Master/Archangel

    Say **Archangel Michael** (or whichever Divine energy you have chosen), **please be with me.**

    Do the following breathing exercises: inhale to the count of four, hold to the count of four and exhale to the count of eight. Do this a total of three times.

2. Say the following prayer:

   Archangel Michael (or whichever Ascended Master/Archangel you have chosen)**, please bring forward all negative thought forms created by me or by other people, that have taken up residence in my energy body. Please dissolve and remove these thought forms from my energy field.**

   Also in the coming days, please help me to shift any behavioural patterns or auric patterns, which support these negative thought forms, and dissolve those too.

   Please replace all of these negative thought forms and behavioural/auric patterns with new ones, which resonate with love, courage, strength, peace, self-love and personal power (or whichever energies are most important to you).

   Thank you. It is done; it is done; it is done.

How Often To Use This Prayer

I use the negative thought form prayer a few times per week. You can do it more or less often, depending on what feels right for you.

Remember that in order to keep your empath gifts in balance, you will need to use these techniques or some other form of energy clearing regularly. Therefore, I recommend incorporating the clearings for removing emotional residues and psychic ties into your daily schedule (I like to do these at the end of the day), and doing the other clearings periodically as needed.

Key Points from Chapter One:

- All human beings sense or experience emotional and psychological data from other people through a variety of mechanisms, such as the mirror neuron system, and coming into contact with other people's electromagnetic fields
- The difference between empaths and non-empaths is that empaths feel this data more vividly, and can in some cases also carry it with them once the experience is over
- For empaths these experiences may accumulate and leave residues in their energy fields, which can leave them feeling energetically burdened or bogged down
- Of all the types of energetic debris that an empath can take on, **Emotional Residues** are perhaps the most common – these can also accumulate in the empath's energy field when he or she is affected by someone else's negative emotions
- Another common type of energetic debris is **Earthbound Spirits** – empaths may take these on when they are experiencing other people's energies, which can drain their own energy and amplify their negative emotions
- Empaths can also feel overly aware of other people's thoughts and feelings through the accumulation of **Psychic Ties**
- **Unwanted Influencing Energy** can affect empaths by making it more difficult to recognise our own needs and

desires. It can block our intuition and sense of clarity in life, even interfering with our free will.

- Empaths can also sometimes pick up **Negative Thought Forms** from other people and their environments – these negative energies can subtly influence us to think in more negative ways.

- It is a good idea for empaths to cleanse their energy fields regularly of the energetic debris that they may accumulate – doing so can help the empath to feel clearer, lighter and more like themselves

- I recommend that empaths clear psychic ties and emotional residues at least a few times per week. The other types of energetic clutter can be cleared less frequently.

- The techniques given in this book work through your spoken intention to release these energies from your own auric field! Your energy field is your own, and you have every right to dismiss any energies that are not yours and which did not originate with you. The Divine-level energies (such as Ascended Masters and Archangels) are there to assist you in the process of clearing them effectively.

Chapter Two

How to Heal Overactive Empathy

In the previous chapter, you learned how to release the energies that all empaths can come across in their day-to-day lives. Clearing out energies that are not yours is extremely important for empaths. But sometimes we are so overwhelmed by these energies, and pick them up so frequently, that we need a solution that goes deeper than just clearing earthbound spirits or emotional residues. That is what this chapter will cover.

So next, I am going to talk about the most common root causes of overactive empathy, and how you can resolve them to bring your empath gifts back into balance, so they can serve your life instead of detracting from it.

But before we can discuss the root causes of overactive empathy, and how we can bring our empath gifts back into balance, we also need to think about how we become empaths in the first place, and how our empath gifts actually get out of balance.

Through my experiences working with many empath clients, I have come to the conclusion that **most empaths are made, not born**. And in this chapter, I am going to explain why, and how this insight is key to recovering from the collection of symptoms I term 'overactive empathy.'

But first, let's look at how a person becomes an empath, and why this matters to the recovery process.

How Does a Person Become An Empath?

Many people are born with empath gifts that are lying dormant. Their empath gifts will often reveal themselves in childhood or adulthood, when a person goes through a particular **event** or encounters a particular **relationship dynamic.**

Let's have a look at the kind of events and relationship dynamics that can trigger us to become empaths.

The first significant trigger, which affects a lot of people, is traumatic life events.

The Role of Trauma

A trauma is an event the mind is unable to process fully at the moment it occurs, due to it being very negative, sudden, and overwhelming. By its very nature, a trauma is something that threatens our survival, or an event we *perceive* to be life threatening.

Undergoing a trauma is effectively like having the rug pulled out from underneath us – it knocks us off our feet, damages our sense of safety in the world, and often undermines our faith or spiritual connection with God or the Universe.

How Traumas Activate Our Latent Empath Gifts

Different people respond to trauma in a variety of ways, according to their temperament and past experiences.

One common way in which trauma can negatively affect us is by weakening our energetic defences against the outside world, and even causing temporary damage to our energetic field. Trauma effectively renders our energy fields more 'porous' by temporarily affecting the integrity of the etheric body. And for those with a predisposition to high empathy, this usually manifests as an activation of our latent empath gifts.

People who have been empaths for as long as they can remember have often been affected by traumas which occurred in their early years.

Below you will find a list of common childhood traumas which can 'switch on' our empath gifts in childhood. Take note of any which sound familiar to you and your life history, and feel free to journal about it, if you have any insights which come to you as you look over the items below.

Common Childhood Traumas Which Can Activate Empath Gifts:

- A premature or difficult birth experience
- Childhood neglect
- Sexual assault/abuse
- Prolonged separation from a parent/primary caregiver

- A distant or emotionally unavailable parent
- Harsh physical discipline and abuse
- The death of a parent or loved one
- Seeing one's parents separate or get divorced (especially if it was acrimonious)
- Frequent moves in childhood
- Undergoing a medical procedure or operation, or a long illness
- Growing up in a home with lots of conflict
- Ongoing relational trauma, which often occurs in situations like being raised by a parent struggling with substance addiction, mental illness, or a personality disorder, such as narcissistic personality disorder or borderline personality disorder.

It is important to note that what may be traumatic for one person may not be for another. For example, one child might take frequent changes of home or school in stride, while another might find the same experiences traumatizing. It all depends on the child's temperament, previous experiences, and in some cases perhaps even her past life wounds (more on this subject later).

Note also that there may be multiple traumas which accumulate to activate our empath gifts.

Other Triggers of Overactive Empathy

Trauma is not the only factor that can cause us to become empaths. The dynamics of our childhood relationships (namely, the ones we have with our parents) can play a big part, too.

Here are some relationship dynamics that can 'switch on' our empath gifts in childhood:

1. Failing to Have Our Needs Met in Infancy

Experience has shown me that a person can become an empath because at some point in childhood, he/she struggled to get one or more fundamental needs met. These needs may include love and affection, attention, physical touch, sensory stimulation, food, or any type of basic care.

How Unmet Childhood Needs Can Activate Our Empath Gifts

Human babies and infants are wired to be **highly attuned** to their parents and caregivers – more so than any other species. This is because young humans have the longest period of dependence for survival on their caregivers out of any species. While many mammals lose their dependence on their parents after several months, humans remain dependent for several years.

Children have both material needs and emotional needs: they need to be fed, clothed and have their basic requirements attended to, and they also need to be engaged with, loved, cuddled, and stimulated in order to develop normally.

Researchers have demonstrated that the results of not getting one's material and emotional needs met in infancy can have life-long consequences. In 2000, Harvard University and Boston Children's Hospital began a study which demonstrated the results of severe neglect and abuse on young children.

As part of their research, they studied the brains of Romanian children who were abandoned to the care of orphanages under Ceaușescu's communist government. Many of these children had suffered severe neglect and abuse, in heartbreaking scenarios where they had been drugged, starved, chained to their cots, or in some cases, left to die.

The study found that the orphans' brain development was impaired as a result of this neglect. In particular, the white matter (the area of the brain which allows neurons to communicate with one another) was greatly impaired, resulting in a low IQ and poor communication skills.

The Relevance of This Discovery For Empaths

The above mentioned study illustrates in real terms how deeply invested infants must be in attracting the material resources of their caregivers, and also in earning their love and attention. The stakes are high, because in failing to get these basic needs met, a child can die or sustain brain damage – ending up socially, emotionally, and psychologically impaired for life.

As a result, babies and small children tend to be highly sensitive on a very primal level to any threats to having their needs fulfilled.

How Children Respond When Their Needs Are Unmet

My work with empaths has shown me that one of the common ways infants and children deal with a threat to their needs being unmet is by **stepping up their level of emotional attunement** to their parent(s) or caregivers.

This causes the infant to develop an even higher level of empathy with their parent, essentially switching the focus from the infant's needs to the parent's needs. Perhaps the logic behind it is the following: "If I tune in to you and try to work out why you are not here for me, perhaps then I can pre-empt your neglect (or even fix it)."

In this way, overactive empathy is an adaptive survival strategy that the infant or child has chosen in an attempt to get her needs met. It is of course a strategy that is futile for infants and toddlers, who have very limited power to fix or influence such a situation, even through such a response.

For older children, tending to the parent's needs and stepping up the emotional attunement in this relationship may, in some cases, result in the child receiving more nurturing than she otherwise would have, although it also sets up negative co-dependent relationship patterns that may affect her later in life.

When Caregivers Fail to Meet Their Children's Needs

When a child gets triggered in a way that causes them to become an empath, this does not necessarily mean that they were parented by an 'unfit' parent. Sometimes it was the case that their caregiver was suffering from a temporary state which interfered with their ability to care for a child, such as post-partum depression, or grief following a loss.

In other cases, a caregiver could have been suffering from something more lasting or serious, such as a severe mental illness, an addiction, or a personality disorder. It is very common for the children of such parents to end up as empaths.

Let's look at another common relationship dynamic which can 'switch on' latent empath gifts:

2. Parent/Child Relationships Involving Inappropriate Boundaries

Many boundaries in life are unseen or invisible, such as those around our personal space, or what we will or will not accept in our lives (i.e.where we 'draw the line') when it comes to things like how we expect to be treated by a partner, or what we will spend our money on.

A child's concept of all these unseen boundaries is mostly formed by observing, and then absorbing like a sponge all of the messages his parents send out about their own personal boundaries over the course of his childhood. In this way, the child forms a sense of what is appropriate behaviour and what is not, based on what his parents will or won't accept for themselves.

The messages that some children absorb may be inappropriate, and may not match the 'norm' of the culture and society that the child lives in. Some of these inappropriate messages can contribute toward overactive empathy.

How Inappropriate Boundary Messages Are Received By Children

This can happen when a parent:

- Violates a child's body through physical abuse
- Violates a child's body through sexual assault or abuse
- Violates a child's personal space in other ways, such as failing to respect a child's need for privacy (they may do this by not allowing their child to shut his bedroom door, or snooping through his things).

When these events occur, the child will revise his concept of where his energetic boundaries should be, so that they match what he has just observed. Children tend not to question what they learn about boundaries. They need to believe that their parents are in the right. This is a healthy, adaptive strategy, because it is simply too unsafe for the child's psyche to become aware of the fact that a parent may be wrong when they are physically and emotionally dependent upon that caregiver.

It is normal for a child to grow up believing that his parents are all-knowing, all-powerful beings who have more power or wisdom than they really do. I remember the exact moment in my teens when I discovered that my parents were just human beings like everybody else, and not the higher beings I had thought they were. In that moment I realized that my parents were 'making it up as they went along,' and did not actually possess the superior wisdom or infallibility that I assumed they had when I was a child.

Because of this, when a child is conditioned to believe that his boundaries should be open, porous, or even non-existent, he does not question it. He learns that it is acceptable for another to intrude on his privacy or violate his sexual energy, to give a couple of examples.

It's important to note that childhood boundary violations that lead to overactive empathy do not have to resemble the kind of very dramatic abuse that might lead a concerned neighbour or friend to contact social services. More subtle intrusions can still have a large impact on the child.

An example of a subtle intrusion happened to my client Christina, whose very religious mother insisted on going through her belongings to check for 'forbidden' reading materials, all through Christina's childhood and even into Christina's early twenties.

A person who has experienced boundary violations will experience the effects of these violations on an energetic level

– they can weaken the energetic field, leading to an activation of any latent empath gifts the person has.

It's no coincidence that those with porous boundaries end up with porous energy fields!

For this reason, people who experienced boundary violations are much more likely to become empaths than those who did not experience these challenges. However, ultimately being an empath is a gift and a tool that can help us deal with our own and others' traumas—once we learn to bring it into balance. We'll talk more about this in Chapter 3.

Now, let's have a look at another dynamic which can contribute to the activating of empath gifts:

3. Early Childhood Relationships Involving Hypervigilance

Hypervigilance means that your senses such as vision, hearing, and smell are heightened to detect any possible threats to your safety and well-being. This is a stressful condition in which hormones such as cortisol and adrenaline are released into the bloodstream, in order to allow you to quickly deal with any threats to your survival. This state can be traced back very far in our evolution, to the time when early humans had to prevent predators from eating them.

Children who are raised in a home where there is abuse often become hypervigilant. The logic behind this response is that if one can 'tune in' to one's parents and their moods sufficiently well, the child can either pre-empt or somehow avoid the abuse. This is yet another survival strategy, which may or may not be effective, depending on the situation.

Hypervigilance does not just occur in response to abuse, however. It can also result wherever there is unpredictable behaviour or a sense of anxiety about how another person is going to behave. It can manifest where there are contradictory or confusing messages in a relationship, particularly positive messages mixed with negative messages such as love and hate (this is a common dynamic in abusive relationships). A frequent way that people refer to hypervigilance is 'walking on eggshells.'

Any scenario where you have had to walk on eggshells for long periods, especially as a child, can predispose a person towards high empathy.

So now we've looked at the dynamics and patterns which can cause us to become empaths.

Here's an example of how some of these factors might combine to cause a person to become an empath:

Rebecca's Experience With Hypervigilance

My client Rebecca's empath gifts were triggered around the age of six, when her father died and her mother went into a period of deep grief that lasted for several years. Rebecca remembers this time as one where her mother was unable to pay her much attention. As a caring and sensitive child, Rebecca would try to bring her mother out of her sadness by creating gifts for her, making her laugh, and putting on theatrical performances for her. These efforts were often unsuccessful, but Rebecca continued to try, and this activated her empathic side.

She went into adulthood with high empathy for others, and was very drawn to people who were suffering. She had two romantic relationships with men who were not able to meet her emotional needs, because they were so consumed by their own suffering. One of these relationships (her second marriage) pushed her into a state of imbalance as an empath that took her a long time to recover from.

Rebecca and her husband Chris had been married for three years when Chris's beloved brother (who was also his closest friend) committed suicide. Chris spiraled into a depression and began to abuse alcohol.

Rebecca essentially became his carer. She took him to the hospital when he hurt himself, tried to stop him from drinking, and provided for both of them financially when Chris lost his job as a result of his drinking problem. She was also his primary emotional support. There were other traumas which occurred during this period, including the miscarriage of a child.

These events kept her in a state of hypervigilance and high attunement to others, to the point of complete energetic overwhelm in her forties. At that time she found she could no longer spend much time with other people, because she was so energetically depleted.

Experience has shown me that Rebecca's energetic overwhelm progressed along a common pattern. Her latent gifts were initially triggered in childhood, then became heightened in adulthood following traumatic events (the chaotic experience of being in a relationship with an addict and the trauma of losing her baby). She then reached a point of almost total depletion in her forties, when she began to work on bringing her empath gifts into balance.

****

How Were Your Empath Gifts Originally Activated?

As mentioned earlier, in my experience, a larger number of people become empaths due to adverse childhood experiences and childhood dynamics. Chances are, if you are an overwhelmed empath, the root causes of this can be found in your early background.

I encourage you to consider your own formative experiences, and in particular whether any of the conditions and patterns mentioned in this chapter were a part of your childhood. For example:

- Physical abuse or punishment (such as hitting or spanking)
- Sexual abuse
- Invasions of privacy or space
- Living amidst chaos or having to 'walk on eggshells' for extended periods

- Having your material or emotional needs neglected
- Any scenarios where your parents' needs were prioritized throughout your childhood, at the expense of yours

A good way into this exercise is to ask yourself: if you were writing your life story, which events or relationships would you include as impactful?

And which (if any) of these events and relationship dynamics might be connected to your empathy?

Please note that you will need some time and thought for this exercise. This is not something you want to rush, so give these ideas a few days to sink into your subconscious mind, and see what comes to the surface over the coming days.

_____

_____

_____

_____

_____

_____

_____

Notes For The Above Exercise:

Reflecting on negative memories can trigger suppressed, strong emotions for some people – this is completely normal and to be expected.

If you find these feelings overwhelming or unbearable, try to re-centre yourself and bring your focus back onto your body. Here are some suggestions to help you do this:

- Spend ten minutes breathing normally through your nose and focusing on the sensation of the air passing in and out of your nostrils
- Go for a walk
- Close your eyes and clench your fists ten times in a row; with every clenching, focus completely on the sensation of your hands being squeezed into fists, breathing normally as you do it

If you find evaluating your childhood experiences provokes a lot of negative feelings, you might also want to enlist the services of a qualified psychotherapist or counsellor to help.

"I DON'T RECOGNISE MYSELF OR MY CHILDHOOD IN ANY OF THE ABOVE!"

Through my work with empaths, I have seen that a small minority of them are indeed just born that way, so the information above does not apply to everyone.

I would recommend that you give the ideas presented in the last section a bit of time to sink in, but if you come to the conclusion that they simply do not apply to you, then you may be interested in Appendix E right at the end of this book. In that segment, I present a few reasons why a person may be born as an empath.

What If You Became An Empath Later in Life?

Some people who complete the exercise above recognise some of the patterns and experiences covered in this chapter as having begun in their adult lives, rather than in childhood.

It is true that the same experiences which cause us to become empaths in childhood can also cause us to become empaths in adulthood. So sometimes a person is born with latent empath gifts that do not become activated until they are in adulthood.

So What Next?

Once you are an empath, you can either become overwhelmed by it, or you can seek to remain in balance. Alternately, you may fluctuate between these two states throughout your lifetime.

Note that the same events and circumstances that **trigger the development of empath gifts in early childhood (or adulthood)** are usually the same ones that can also cause one's empath gifts to become out of balance, and may tip a person into a state of energetic overwhelm in adulthood.

For that reason, if you identified as an **'overwhelmed empath'** at the beginning of this book, you will want to pay attention to what I cover next – the solutions to 'overactive empathy.'

Note: if you identified as a balanced empath at the beginning of this book, the following information may not apply to you, and you may wish to skip ahead to Chapter Three.

Chapter Two, Part Two

Methods for Reducing Overactive Empathy

At this point, we've covered the various ways in which our empath gifts can get 'switched on,' usually in childhood.

Once we are empaths, we cannot 'unbecome' empaths – none of us can go back in time and change the triggers that activated our gifts in the first place.

But what we CAN do is take actions to ensure we remain in balance with our empath gifts once they are activated. That is what this section is all about.

(As an aside, I am hoping that once you've finished the final chapter in this book, you will understand more fully why these gifts are valuable, and will not want to surrender your hard-earned empath gifts anyway)!

How to Bring Overactive Empathy Back Into Balance

There are two ways in which I have seen empaths come back into balance after being chronically overwhelmed by their empathy.

The first is to **minimize and/or heal 'empath-triggering relationships.'** The second is to **release traumas**.

Let's have a look at the first one:

What Is An Empath-Triggering Relationship?

An empath-triggering relationship is one that activates and then aggravates your empathy, causing it to go out of balance. These relationships can sometimes be abusive in nature, although not always.

Here are some key features of empath-triggering relationships:

You are hyper-attuned to the needs of the other person, while having your own needs ignored or minimized

As Rebecca's story with her grieving mother in the last section of this chapter illustrates, we can often end up as empaths because the relationship we had with one of our primary caregivers did not meet our basic needs. As a result, we developed a strategy of hyper-attunement to our caregiver in order to deal with this – a strategy that caused us to minimize our needs and focus on the needs of our parent(s). Often, we unconsciously take these co-dependent childhood dynamics into our adult relationships, perpetuating a negative cycle that increases empathic overwhelm.

Here are some examples of adult relationships with a co-dependent aspect to them:

- Gemma has a friend who is always talking about her problems, but isn't interested in hearing about Gemma's life.
- Tom's sister is irresponsible with money and constantly asks to borrow money from him. Tom has a low income and gets into credit card debt to help his sister.
- Valerie repeatedly allows her spouse to make decisions for the family (such as where to live) that benefit him, but he doesn't take her needs or desires into account at all.

These patterns, which involve prioritizing other people's needs at one's own expense, are not uncommon among empaths. This is because empaths are giving people who care deeply about others, and they often do not consider whether they are receiving the same care, consideration, or attention in return.

Let's have a look at the second type of empath-triggering relationship which can aggravate our empath gifts in adulthood:

Relationships involving mixed messages or frightening interactions

I mentioned earlier on in this book that living in a state of hypervigilance can activate our empath gifts in childhood. But hypervigilance doesn't just affect us in childhood – it can also heighten our empath gifts if we experience it in our adult relationships.

Relationships that trigger a sense of hypervigilance may feature situations such as being criticized, verbally attacked, or generally feeling unsafe around someone. This can also occur when trust is lacking, or a person's behaviour does not 'add up' or make sense. If a person's words and actions don't align, this can be triggering as well.

To give an example of this, let's say that you have a friend who reacts angrily when things do not go her way, and takes her anger out on the people around her. When confronted about it, she denies it and does not take responsibility for her behaviour.

Such dynamics are often present in emotionally abusive relationships. But really any dynamic that has you walking on eggshells, wondering what kind of negative experience or interaction is waiting around the corner for you, can cause your empathy to go into overdrive.

There is a third type of relationship which can aggravate empathy in adulthood:

Relationships where the other person does not take responsibility for themselves

Empaths can be highly triggered by people who are suffering. This includes those who are chronically negative, and people who take on a 'victim' role in their lives, by handing their power and responsibility for their lives over to other people. People who complain a lot and seem perpetually "stuck in a rut" in their jobs, and relationships can sometimes fit into this category.

Disempowered or unhappy people can trigger empaths in a few different ways.

First of all, empaths hate to see others suffer, and they often want to heal others of their problems. Such people activate our desire to help, and cause us to want to extend our energy field to carry them on our backs, energetically (and sometimes practically) speaking. 'I wish I could help you!' we think. The other person may buy into the idea that only someone else can create change for them. We may forget that everyone is connected to Source energy or God. Others can access their personal power, and the ability to create change through this connection. We cannot invite others to connect to Source through us – this will only drain us and fail to help the other person.

But when another person invites us to take responsibility for something that is not ours to take on, this can trigger a co-dependent pattern in us, where we take the focus off ourselves and our own lives, and focus excessively on other people and their problems. In situations like these, some empaths become confused energetically about what is and isn't theirs to deal with. They may carry someone else's emotional residue energies (such as helplessness or fear) around with them. The more we identify with another person's problems in life, the more porous we may feel on the energetic level.

It is worth noting that we often re-enact childhood co-dependent patterns in our adult relationships in order to create a different outcome "this time." Therefore, becoming aware of and changing these patterns goes a long way towards healing our childhood wounds.

There is another way that our empath gifts can go into overdrive:

Relationships where boundaries are unclear or frequently violated

In childhood and in adulthood, poor boundaries in our personal relationships can weaken our energetic boundaries. The physical plane is directly connected to the spiritual/energetic plane. Having good boundaries in the physical world strengthens our energetic field, and causes it to be less porous. Therefore, being aware of where our boundaries lie is extremely important for empaths. Equally important is verbalizing what is and is not acceptable for us, thus ensuring that others respect our boundaries.

Those of us who became empaths as a result of boundary violations in childhood are often triggered by unclear or frequently violated boundaries in adulthood.

This was true for my client Melanie, who was a highly sought-after empathic healer with a long waiting list of clients. She also had a cancellation policy that she never enforced.

When a client cancelled their appointment without 24 hours notice, or failed to show up altogether, Melanie was out of pocket, but felt shy about asking for her cancellation fee. This caused her to feel angry and resentful toward a few of her clients, who regularly cancelled or rescheduled appointments without proper notice. Her important boundary in the physical plane (which was not being tended to) was mirrored in the energetic plane, heightening Melanie's empathy.

Do You Have Any Empath-Triggering Relationships in Your Life?

The dynamics of our relationships are such a major factor in our emotional health and balance as empaths. For this reason, evaluating our relationships (both personal and professional), and identifying any that may be triggering us are important steps which can help us to come back into balance.

Exercise: Make a list of your close relationships and your acquaintanceships, and take note of any that may be 'empath-triggering' connections.

Below I have listed some common indications that a relationship is an empath-triggering one. The more of these points you can tick off for a particular relationship, the more likely it is that the connection is heightening your empathic side.

Signs of an Empath-Triggering Relationship:

- You consistently find the connection draining
- You often feel dominated – the other person has lots of ideas and opinions about how you should live your life (think: unwanted influencing energy)
- She frequently criticizes you or other people
- She frequently blames you for her mistakes

- You often feel the connection is shallow, as she does not open up to you emotionally or show any vulnerability
- She often acts like a victim
- When you are with her, you usually listen more than you talk
- She emphasizes her needs and doesn't seem to care about your needs
- You have the sense that she sees you primarily as a means to get what she wants
- You suspect that she doesn't think highly of you, or respect you
- Your needs, ideas and suggestions (such as where to go to dinner together) are often disregarded or dismissed
- You are often accused of being 'too sensitive' when you stand up for yourself
- You feel infantilized (i.e. like a 5 year old) when you are around her – she talks down to you
- You often feel like you 'are supposed' to ask permission from her to do things that normally you would not have to ask permission for
- She often points out your flaws and shortcomings
- She rarely or never apologizes when she is in the wrong
- She repeatedly steps over your boundaries and ignores your requests for limits
- She is not there for you emotionally even though you are there for her

- She threatens to end the relationship in order to get her way
- You often feel angry around her
- On balance, the relationship is not a source of peace or fulfillment, and causes you more anguish or trouble than it contributes positive aspects to your life.

When You Have an Empath-Triggering Relationship in Your Life

Realizing that someone we care about is contributing to our heightened empathy can take us by surprise. But there are some solutions here:

Depending on the behaviour and the dynamics that are triggering you, you can either work with the other person to shift the old dynamic into something that is more beneficial for you, or you can minimize or avoid contact with the other person altogether.

Many relationships are not ones that we necessarily want to end, so it is often worthwhile to attempt to change your role in the dynamic, and transform the connection into something healthier. But of course this is something that is not entirely within our control – it also requires the conscious participation of the other party.

To this end, it can be useful to ask yourself:

- **How are your needs not being met in this situation?**
- **How are you contributing to this dynamic?**

- **What can you do differently in future?**

Let's look at the example of Tom, who has a sister who uses him like an ATM. Tom could reiterate that he is here for her in other ways, but that he no longer has the means to bail her out.

As for Gemma's friend who does a lot of talking but doesn't care to listen to her, Gemma could share this observation, and state that she feels neglected and unheard in the friendship.

How Do You Know If A Relationship Can Be Transformed into One That Does Not Trigger You as an Empath?

When you express your insights about the relationship (i.e. that you want to change the dynamic), the other person needs to be at least somewhat open to what you are telling them. They also must be willing and able to work on the relationship. They must show that they value their connection with you.

When you ask another person to help change an unhealthy dynamic in your relationship, there is unfortunately always a chance that they will refuse to participate in this process.

When this happens, and you know that there is not much possibility for change, we need to take people at their word. Reducing or avoiding contact is often a good option in such situations. This is of course easier to do when the person in question is somebody you see once or twice per year, like a distant relative. It is not so easy to do when this is someone who is a part of your daily life, such as your spouse, parent or a co-worker.

It is of course a valid choice to continue the relationship as it is. But in my experience, and in that of my clients, if you have an empath-triggering relationship in your life and the dynamics of that relationship do not change, it is unlikely that you will succeed in reducing your overactive empathy to a significant degree.

If you decide to renegotiate relationship dynamics, reduce contact or eliminate someone from your life altogether, all of these choices require courage and can be messy. Cutting contact with a person should obviously be a last resort, but it is also a choice that can be very liberating and healing, especially if you have a pattern of relationships like this going back to your childhood.

I have had clients who have let go of their marriages or important family relationships upon realizing that the dynamics of those relationships were unhealthy or toxic, and that there was absolutely no willingness from the other person to work on repairing them.

In such relationships, heightened empathy tended not to be the only indicator that something had gone awry for the client. Often the unequal or challenging dynamics created stress that manifested in other ways too, sometimes causing health problems.

I do not wish to minimize the consequences (and potential gains) that come from taking this kind of action. Cutting contact with important people in our lives - people who are abusive or deeply unhealthy - is a difficult path, but one that can also bring us greater healing, peace, and wholeness. You will know in your heart if that is a path that you need to walk.

Next, I want to share a story from one of my clients who was able to reduce her overactive empathy rather easily by minimizing contact with certain family members.

Catherine's In-Laws

Every Thanksgiving, Catherine's in-laws descended on her and her husband. She dreaded it, because her father-in-law was a very combative person. He and Catherine's brother-in-law often got into arguments that would end badly and upset everyone present. Catherine's empathy was always highly triggered during this visit, and she was left feeling exhausted after the family had left.

The fact was that she no longer wanted to spend the holidays in their company, but her husband wouldn't hear of it. They were at an impasse.

Eventually, Catherine took control of the situation by setting a strong boundary, and told her husband she was booking a holiday overseas for Thanksgiving. He could either come with her, or he could stay home and entertain his family on his own. She knew he might not accept her decision, but that was not her problem any longer.

He finally chose to accompany her, and they enjoyed the holiday so much that they are doing the same thing this year. Catherine has since found that taking the relatively simple step of refusing to host her husband's family for the holidays has helped to reduce her overactive empathy.

Empaths need to be surrounded by emotionally healthy people in order to be in a state of balance.

This is something that all empaths should be aware of, as we meet new people and make choices about who we want in our lives. As caring, sensitive, responsible, and ethical people who often give others the benefit of the doubt repeatedly, empaths have a greater propensity to unconsciously choose or tolerate:

- People who don't take responsibility for their lives or actions
- Bullies and abusers
- People who seek to engage in one-sided relationships
- Those who have untreated personality disorders

For this reason, it really benefits us to be very selective about who we let into our lives.

If you should come across an empath-triggering person and you recognize it before you become entangled, the very best thing you can do, in my experience, is remove yourself from the situation and move on.

Practicing these boundaries can go a long way toward balancing our empathy. However, sometimes we achieve balanced empathy only to get taken by surprise when our empathy becomes overactive again. There is a way to deal with this.

When Your Heightened Empathy Makes a Comeback

As mentioned earlier in this book, I managed to reduce my overactive empathy in a big way, but a few years ago, a strange thing happened – my heightened empathy returned! Through this experience, I learned a lot about how our empathy gets re-triggered.

Here's what happened:

I was visiting Western Massachusetts in January, and I rented an Airbnb room for several nights.

Problems emerged immediately. It was extremely cold in my room, but the owner refused to put the central heating temperature up. Eventually, after a few nights, she found me a space heater, but she put strict limits on where and when it could be used. I ignored those limits in order to stay warm, but felt hypervigilant about it.

My empathy was triggered in this situation, mostly because my needs were not being met, whereas the host's need for control was. This paralleled the relationship I had with my mother, which had triggered my empath gifts in the first place.

The host was also highly anxious, and I had the sense she was going to lose her temper at any moment. This further increased my sense of hypervigilance in the situation (again, an element of my relationship with my mother).

Another insightful empath was living in the house at the same time, and she told me she felt her empathy was also being triggered by this woman. She began seeking an alternative living arrangement because of it.

The reason I shared this story is to illustrate that we can sometimes have encounters which trigger us temporarily, and cause us to fall back into disempowering patterns that were a part of our childhood. Pay attention if your empathy comes back into balance, but then flares up in a particular interaction or scenario - it is usually a reflection of the dynamics of the situation you're currently in, or the person you are dealing with.

Once the situation is over, the trigger should die down, and your empath gifts should come back into balance.

****

So now we've looked at the changes we can make to our relationships to reduce overactive empathy. Next, let's look at the second way we can come back into balance with our empath gifts, which is through releasing past traumatic experiences.

How to Identify Past Traumatic Experiences

I mentioned earlier in this chapter that traumas can cause the energetic field to become porous, so our empath gifts can be switched on in the first place by traumas we experience in infancy and childhood.

For some empaths, traumatic events occur in childhood, activating their latent empath gifts, and then further traumas may occur in later life to aggravate their empathy further, pushing them into a state of energetic overwhelm in adulthood.

For other people, there are no signs of their empath gifts in childhood, but a heightened empathy suddenly emerges in adulthood, usually as a result of a trauma. Sometimes there may be repeated traumas in adulthood, until the final one comes along and is the straw that breaks the camel's back, so to speak.

No matter how trauma might manifest, though, it has been for many of my clients a huge factor in developing heightened empathy. To bring empath gifts back into balance, one must often consider the part that trauma has played in one's life story.

Below is an example list of traumas (many of which have been the 'final straw' for my clients).

Examples of Traumatic Life Events

- Being physically assaulted
- Being raped or sexually abused
- Being involved in, or witnessing a serious accident (or the aftermath thereof)
- Losing your job
- Losing your home
- Being cheated on or betrayed
- Being diagnosed with a serious illness
- A loved one being diagnosed with a serious illness

- Being emotionally/psychologically abused
- Losing a loved one
- Losing a beloved pet
- Having a serious adverse reaction to a medication
- Going into anaphylactic shock
- Having a difficult birth
- Going through a divorce
- Having a near-death experience
- Witnessing an assault or a murder
- Having a miscarriage
- Experiencing a natural disaster (such as an earthquake, hurricane, flood or fire)
- Experiencing or witnessing a terrorist attack
- Having an abortion
- Losing your income or going bankrupt
- Living in a warzone
- Being bullied in the workplace

Identifying your past traumas is another important step for bringing your empath gifts back into balance. So, for this next exercise, I am going to ask you make a note of any of the examples given above that reflect your life experiences.

A few notes on this exercise:

There is no concrete list of things that will definitely be traumatic for everyone. People are traumatized by different experiences, and this is why it can be so tricky to know if our experiences constituted 'trauma.' So be open to the fact that yours may not be listed above, and accept that if it felt like a trauma for you, it likely was one.

Nor do our traumas always come from experiencing negative events first hand – for example, many people were traumatized by viewing footage of the 9/11 terrorist attacks on television, to give one prominent example. Just because a trauma did not happen to you directly does not mean you were not affected by it.

Sometimes our traumas are 'relational traumas' which occur in interactions with other people (often bullies or abusers), in an ongoing way.

Brigitte's Ongoing Trauma

My client Brigitte is a good example of someone who experienced ongoing trauma. Brigitte was an A-student at the top of her class, but for some reason when she reached 7th grade, her new form teacher took a dislike to her, and began to make her life hell for no apparent reason. Brigitte's form teacher was also her English teacher, and gave her poor grades in English when she was getting high grades in all her other subjects. She was mocked and humiliated by this teacher in front of the class. She was also repeatedly blamed and punished for things she had not done.

This pattern culminated in Brigitte being accused of bullying another student by her form teacher. The bullying was actually perpetrated by a girl who was in Brigitte's friendship group, but not by her personally.

Brigitte was shamed in front of her class for something she had not done, and she was so upset and angry about it that she could not get the words out to defend herself, and actually blacked out for a moment.

She became so used to being bullied by the teacher that when she reached adulthood, it took her a long time to realize how much she had been affected by this experience of being abused in an ongoing way.

This is just another reminder that identifying your past traumatic experiences is an exercise that can trigger strong, negative emotions for some people.

If you find the feelings overwhelming or unbearable, use some of the suggestions in the last chapter to centre yourself and bring your energy back into your body:

- Spend ten minutes breathing normally through your nose and focusing on the sensation of the air passing in and out of your nostrils
- Go for a walk
- Close your eyes, and clench your fists 10 times in a row - with every clenching, focus completely on the sensation of your hands being squeezed into a fist, breathing normally as you do it

Signs You Are Being Affected By Trauma

Recognizing our own traumas can be tricky. It is natural not to want to revisit events that have caused us pain. In my experience, the unconscious mind will often seek to divert our attention away from that which has hurt us. Therefore, we need to be smart when considering our history, and make sure that we are not subconsciously avoiding areas that have contributed to our heightened empathy.

Here are some signs that you may be carrying an unhealed trauma around a past event:

- Your mind goes blank when you try to think of a specific past occurrence – you have the sense that you want to avoid it, or you have a lot of resistance towards thinking about it
- You still have repeated, upsetting memories or thoughts about a past experience
- You have nightmares about it
- You sometimes avoid places, people, activities or situations that remind you of that experience
- You suffer from unexplained physical symptoms that began following a stressful event, such as gastrointestinal problems, aches and pains, fibromyalgia, or chronic fatigue
- You feel withdrawn from life, or distant from other people
- Your present somehow feels dominated by your past
- You often feel powerless

- You suffer from insomnia
- You suffer from depression
- You suffer or have suffered from 'adrenal fatigue'
- You suffer from hypervigilance – you often feel jumpy and 'on edge'
- You have a preoccupation with death and/or loss – you frequently have fearful thoughts or imaginings about losing loved ones or other good things in your life
- You often feel 'spacey' or ungrounded.

Dreams & Trauma

One helpful way to identify traumas that may be contributing to over-active empathy is to look at the dreams you have when you're stressed. Sometimes there can be a specific scenario that plays out repetitively in our dreams which has its roots in a past trauma. So, pay attention to negative repetitive dreams – they sometimes reveal the traumas that we carry. This is something I learned from first-hand experience.

Post-Exam Trauma

For ten years, I had a repetitive dream where I was back at University doing my final exams for my languages degree. In the dream, I had to learn every word in the French and Spanish dictionaries, and I only had a few months to do it. I felt a sense of panic and hopelessness, as the weight of this impossible task crushed me.

In reality, ten years ago, I did my final exams at University for my degree course. About 85% of my final grade came from grueling exams that took place in the final two weeks. It was not possible to re-take the exams in the event of doing badly. My degree was in French and Spanish, and I felt overwhelmed by the sheer amount of vocabulary I had to learn for the translation part of my exam, which of course had to be done without a dictionary.

Although in the end my exams went OK, I did end up traumatized by the whole experience. The trauma gave me nightmares for a decade, and I developed a bad case of repetitive strain injury (RSI) in my arms and hands that took me years to fully recover from.

This is a good example of how our dreams can nudge us towards healing a difficult past experience. It also illustrates quite well how different people end up traumatized by different events. Clearly not everybody who took those exams would have ended up traumatized for years afterwards. I was particularly vulnerable to being traumatized by exam pressure due to my perfectionistic nature, my unhealed childhood traumas, and my relationships with my parents.

Trauma & The Mind Body Relationship

Once we have an idea of what traumatized us, we want to know—what can we do about it?

Before I cover the topic of healing traumas, it is important to look at how the body and mind are impacted by trauma. This knowledge has great relevance to the healing process.

Trauma & the Work of Dr. Peter Levine

Dr. Levine is a renowned trauma and stress scholar who has researched the effects of trauma on mammals.

In his studies, he found that animals that spend their lives surrounded by predators show no signs of being traumatized. This is because when a traumatic event occurs, the 'stress chemicals' such as adrenaline that are produced by being in danger are actually used up during the fight or flight process.

In addition, the skeletal muscle contraction that naturally occurs when a mammal is in danger is 'shaken out' afterwards (if the animal survives, of course). This happens through physical shaking and trembling movements. In this way, the fear energy has a chance to be processed and discharged through the animal's nervous system right after the trauma occurs.

This is why people (and animals) shake when they are afraid or in shock. These shaking movements are an innate mechanism to release the fear, tension and adrenaline that course through our bodies when we're afraid or traumatized.

Animals shake freely following traumas, but humans tend to inhibit these movements because we often do not want other people to see us so frightened and vulnerable. We may numb our reactions by having a stiff drink. Or we may tell ourselves to stop shaking and get it together.

So what happens when we suppress natural shaking reactions?

When we do not release the adrenaline, tension and fear generated by traumatic events, these can get stored deep in our skeletal muscles, and these muscles remain in a state of chronic contraction. So even though the traumatic event might have passed, the tension generated by the event and stored in the muscles, signaling to the body that we are still in danger.

The body responds by raising the levels of stress hormones in the body, such as cortisol and adrenaline. The nervous system, in its 'activated' state, may also get triggered by sights, smells, sounds and other stimuli reminiscent of the original event, which can result in symptoms such as flashbacks and nightmares. These often occur because memories of traumatic events tend to be poorly integrated into our minds.

Trauma & Memory

Normally, when we experience an event, the brain perceives the event as a bunch of data, and sends this data to an area of the brain that processes stimuli and connects memories and feelings to past sensations. This is how we learn to recognize things. We learn not to touch a hot stove because we remember that we touched it once before and got burned. We extracted meaning from the experience, and made a mental note that it is not good to touch hot stoves.

But when a traumatic experience occurs, we experience it differently. Our brains get so overwhelmed by this awful event that we can't take it in, and the stimuli is not processed fully. Our brains fail to attach the memories and sensations that we felt to the specific event. Bits of memories are instead stored in the unconscious mind as pictures, feelings and sounds, and these are the unresolved memories that can be triggered later on. We do not yet have a cohesive story that we can make out of what happened. Instead, it is a frightening jumble of memories that still doesn't make sense, and affects how we respond in our present lives. And this can cause us to perceive danger where there is none.

I have experienced this phenomenon myself.

I was living in the city centre of Christchurch, New Zealand when the city was devastated by a massive earthquake in 2011. For many months after this event, my instinct was to run for cover every time I heard a lorry going past on the road outside my house, because I thought it was another earthquake. It took me months to understand that I had been traumatized. I wish I had had more information about trauma back then.

The more you understand the effects of trauma, the easier it is to process what has happened to you, and to recover from it. We definitely do not want to carry the remnants of trauma in our nervous system on an ongoing basis. Those who do not recover from trauma suffer more - not just with overactive empathy, but with physical and mental health issues.

Believe it or not, being traumatized can also shape our future, setting in motion a powerful domino effect that means we're more likely to encounter further negative or traumatic events if we do not heal.

There are two reasons for this:

1. When we are traumatized, we are more likely to make poor decisions

Trauma victims tend to make decisions from the part of their brain that is triggered and in 'reactive' mode. This is the **reptilian part of the brain** that has been around for millions of years. Survival depends on the avoidance of pain and the repetition of pleasure, and so it is the reptilian part of our brains that has the job of keeping us away from possible pain and/or death – for example, causing us to run from a predator when we are in danger.

This is not the part of the brain that we normally use to make decisions (unless we have been traumatized), because it is very reactive.

Most of the time, humans utilize their neocortex in decision making, because this is the part of the brain that is responsible for logic and reasoning. This part of our brain looks at a choice from a rational standpoint, taking in all the information available, and coming to a sound conclusion that usually benefits us.

However, when we come at a decision from a traumatized place, the reptilian area of the brain (and more specifically the limbic system, which is the part of the brain that controls our emotions and fight/flight response) kicks in, and causes us to make decisions based on our emotions at the time.

When we are making decisions in this state of mind, it usually causes us to make poor choices – emotional or impulsive ones that we have not thought through, and which often have unintended negative consequences.

For example, my client Jessica had a difficult and traumatic childhood which involved moving from place to place with her mother, trying to escape her violent father who was stalking her mother. This caused a lot of trauma for Jessica, and she made choices later on in her life from a reactive, emotional place. When her limbic system kicked in, it took her back to that place in her childhood where she felt powerless to affect any change in her life, and opportunities to improve her situation were non-existent.

As a result, she made choices from that place of powerlessness, and saw no way out. This resulted in her repeatedly choosing unsafe housing and living situations. Her unconscious belief was that she had no other options.

The trauma in Jessica's childhood effectively caused a spiral of reactive decision making, until eventually she became homeless. By that point, her limbic system was so activated that her situation seemed impossible to change, at least to her mind.

If we have experienced traumas earlier on in our lives, we often find ourselves in similar situations later on - attracting more of what we have already had. The effects of those poor decisions can be hard to undo, and it can be difficult to catch a break - we may even feel trapped or cursed.

It is clear that trauma can affect what shows up in our lives in the long term, in a very uncanny (and often horrible) way.

The second reason that traumatized people are likely to encounter further traumas if they don't heal is the following:

2. When we are carrying something unresolved and unprocessed in our psyche, we naturally seek resolution for it by being attracted to similar events

This is what Freud referred to as the **'repetition compulsion.'** The human psyche has an in-built drive to heal and recover from past traumas. In a bid to make sense of traumatic memories, the psyche actually seeks out aspects of the trauma in order to re-play them – as a result, it is prone to remaining stuck in the trauma.

To give one common example, people who grow up with abusive parents in childhood will often be drawn to abusive partners later on. By being drawn to a similar energy or dynamic later on, the mind seeks to resolve or somehow change the outcome of the original traumatic experience.

This also means that if we have had difficult experiences in childhood which have activated our empathy, we often unconsciously seek out those similar experiences in adulthood, which serves to heighten our empathy even further.

This is why it is important for empaths to heal their traumas.

So just to recap, here's a summary of how trauma affects us:

- When we get traumatised, our skeletal muscles contract. If we do not allow ourselves to tremble and shake following a traumatic event, our muscles will remain chronically contracted and tense.

- Our brains, failing to process the overwhelming data that it was faced with at the time, has only taken in fragments of memories, and has not yet fully made sense of what happened.

- This means that the nervous system, when it comes across something even slightly reminiscent of these memories, imagines itself to be back in the traumatizing situation – it pumps out adrenaline, contracts the skeletal muscles, and flicks the 'Warning – danger!' switch inside our nervous system.

- A psychological phenomenon called the 'repetition compulsion' actually means we may unconsciously seek out similar traumatic events or relationships in the future in a bid to resolve and process what has happened to us in the past. We often keep repeating the same old circumstances that caused the original trauma, until we heal.

The power of old traumas can actually look, and feel like the hand of destiny in our lives – but in reality what is driving us is our compulsion to heal old events by replaying them over and over until we 'get it right.'

In the next section, I'm going to talk about how we can heal traumas to bring overactive empathy back into a state of balance.

Healing from Trauma

In order to heal from trauma, we must:

1. Find a way to process and integrate the fragmented memories of the original traumatizing event
2. Work with the physical body to releasing the tension and fear that is stored in the muscles.

Therefore, the modalities I recommend for trauma and overactive empathy recovery are for the most part **body-based therapies** (to help the body to release traumatic tension) and **talk therapies** (that help our brains to organize the fragmented memories into a story that makes sense). A combination of these two can be very effective.

Now let's look at the most effective modalities out there for trauma:

Trauma Releasing Exercises (TRE)

TRE (Trauma Releasing Exercises) are DIY trauma recovery exercises that help discharge muscular tension in the body following a traumatic experience. They were created by trauma specialist David Berceli, and they combine techniques from yoga, Tai Chi, bioenergetics, and martial arts practices.

As mentioned earlier, shaking and trembling are natural responses to traumatic events, enabling us to release our fear and adrenaline. TRE artificially induce these trembling movements in the human body, helping to release any tension that is residing in the muscles as a result of stressful or traumatic events.

TRE can be used to heal a sole instance of trauma that one is aware of, or these exercises can be used on a more regular basis to release stress and tension that has built up over time.

I recommend them for all empaths who suffer from overactive empathy, and also for those who are in a state of balance. As empaths, we are very susceptible to being traumatized vicariously, through hearing about or seeing others' traumas.

To find out more about these exercises for releasing trauma, check out David Berceli's book: *Trauma Releasing Exercises (TRE): A Revolutionary New Method for Stress & Trauma Recovery*.

(Just a note that I have no affiliation with this author or his work – it is simply a resource that my clients and I personally have found both useful and inexpensive for trauma recovery).

Somatic Experiencing

This healing method was pioneered by the above mentioned Dr. Peter Levine, following his research into the stress response in animals and humans.

In a Somatic Experiencing session, the client is guided to access and release trapped trauma/stress energy by tuning in to the physical sensations that she feels in her body, such as coldness, tightness or tingling. The aim of SE is also to expand awareness of how our mind and body responds in certain stressful situations, and help to create healthier response patterns to stress.

Here is a description of what happens during an Somatic Experiencing session from the Somatic Experiencing website:

"Typically, you will sit comfortably opposite your therapist, be given time to settle, and then asked what issue you'd like to work with.

You'll then be guided to consciously explore – without judgment – related physical sensations, feelings, thoughts and images as they arise.

Through this simple moment-to-moment process – called tracking – it's possible for highly charged stress energy in your body to be properly engaged and released naturally. Examples of this discharge include tingling, warmth, and involuntary muscle movements such as twitching or yawning.

The result of this often subtle mobilisation can be immediate; the trapped survival energy at the root of your symptoms is freed, allowing a new relaxation to establish deep in your body and mind."

This is a modality that is completely focused on releasing traumatic stress, and one that many of my clients have had success with.

You can find the website and practitioners at: TraumaHealing.org

EMDR

EMDR (Eye Movement Desensitization and Reprocessing) is a type of psychotherapy created by Dr. Francine Shapiro that works with memory and the mind. Dr. Shapiro created this technique when she found that she was able to release her traumatic memories effectively by making certain eye movements while thinking about them.

Many of my clients have found this healing method very effective for releasing traumatic experiences.

The EMDR website is at: EMDRIA.org

Craniosacral Therapy

Craniosacral therapy is a type of body work that brings healing through the use of light touch applied to the skull, pelvis and spine. This form of therapy was created by an American physician, Dr. William Garner Sutherland, in the early 1900s. Dr. Sutherland trained as an osteopath, and when working with patients, he found that he was sensing or 'hearing' a subtle movement and rhythmic pattern in the body that reminded him of 'breathing' – except it did not utilize the lungs.

Dr. Sutherland also found, when examining the joints and bones of the skull, that the skull is perfectly designed for these subtle 'inhaling' and 'exhaling' movements. Another of his discoveries was that traumatic events and physical injuries have the effect of hindering this internal rhythm. By utilizing therapeutic touch, Craniosacral therapy helps to release these restrictions in the body caused by traumas so that the body can 'breathe again.'

Craniosacral therapy is especially recommended for traumas that involved physical injury.

Cord Cutting

Cord cutting means cutting an energetic cord with somebody.

What are energetic cords?

An energy cord is an astral-level structure that links you to another person. This is a **negative cord** which contains energetic echoes of the negative aspects of the relationship – you contribute negative patterns into that cord, and the other person does too. Thus the energies of the cord enter your aura, sending negative patterns of thought, emotion and behaviour back and forth between you both. These negative patterns can affect you in your life and in your other relationships.

Let's say for example that Sandra had a partner who cheated on her. Ever since then, she has felt less secure, and she brings that sense of insecurity into her current relationship. That insecurity exists not just emotionally, or psychologically – it also has an energetic component which can affect Sandra too, in the form of the energy cord.

On a psychological level, cord cutting can help people to process stressful and traumatic events, situations, and relationships and move forward with their lives. On a spiritual/energetic level, it helps to release traumas and stuck energies from the auric field.

For this reason, cord cutting is most often recommended for breakups, estrangements, losses, and for relationships which involved traumatic elements such as bullying, abuse or betrayal.

Cord cutting is offered via my website. Practitioners with a background in shamanic healing often practise cord cutting as well.

If you work with a cord cutting practitioner, ensure that the session involves an exploration or discussion of the dynamics and energies contained within the cord. To cut a cord properly and benefit from the healing, we must learn the lessons from our relationships.

Many cord cutting practitioners are actually simply cutting the psychic ties I discussed in Chapter One, which can re-attach soon after they have been cut. If your cord cutting session is very short and only involves requesting that the cords be cut, you most likely have not cut an energetic cord – you've probably cut psychic ties instead.

Psychotherapy & Counselling

Psychotherapy and counselling can help us to understand, process and integrate our past traumatic experiences. Talking about past experiences with a compassionate witness can validate for us that something damaging did indeed happen to us, and that it negatively impacted our sense of safety, empowerment and trust in the world. In some cases, it can be hard to move forward without this sense of external validation.

In order for psychotherapy to be effective, it is important to find a psychotherapist you like, and with whom you feel a connection.

Taking Care of Your Adrenals

The adrenal glands are small glands that sit just above our kidneys. Their job is to produce adrenaline in stressful situations, to enable us to fight or flee. However, when we are carrying trauma, we end up pumping out more adrenaline than we need, and this can tire out the adrenal glands, leave us in a state of 'adrenal fatigue.'

If you have been traumatized, it is important for your recovery to take steps to soothe and replenish your adrenals.

Here are some suggestions for activities and practices for doing this:

- Eat regular meals
- Reduce sugar and caffeine, which are stimulants
- Go to bed and get up at the same time each day
- Rest when you are tired
- Create an emergency fund, and ensure your finances are on a solid footing, as always being broke prolongs the stress/trauma response by activating the limbic system of the brain (the part which is activated when we feel under threat). Soothe the limbic system (and your adrenals) by giving yourself a bit of a financial cushion, as much as is possible.
- Avoid activities which will startle or frighten you, such as scary or violent movies, television or news items
- Top up your nutrient levels, as prolonged periods of stress deplete our nutrient levels, particularly magnesium, the B vitamins, zinc, calcium, vitamin E, and vitamin C. Make sure you eat plenty of foods which contain these nutrients, or talk to a naturopath or doctor to get your nutrient levels checked or supplemented.

Which Type of Trauma Therapy is Right for You?

I often recommend that empaths start with TRE (trauma releasing exercises). There are two reasons for this:

1. It is not always clear to empaths whether their overactive empathy is being caused or aggravated by stored traumas. David Berceli's book enables you to try out the exercises to see if you could benefit from them, without a large monetary investment.

2. Sometimes our traumas occurred before the age of three (i.e. pre-memory traumas), or we do not realise we have been traumatised at some other point in our lives. TRE allows us to release the stored tension from previous traumas, even if we're not sure what they were.

Berceli states that these exercises are not right for everyone, especially those with previous injuries or chronic illness. Read his disclaimer notice before trying out any of the exercises.

If you feel in need of support on your healing path, you may like to try a modality that is administered by a practitioner or a healer instead. Personally I have tried (and benefited from) TRE, Craniosacral therapy, cord cutting, EMDR and psychotherapy.

You may also need to try more than one modality, in order to find the one(s) that are right for you. The path to healing is not always straight or quick, so please don't give up if you don't get what you need from one therapy.

Choosing a Trauma Therapist

The relationship with a trauma practitioner/therapist matters - you need to feel sufficiently safe in the presence of the practitioner, so that your body is able to release any traumas it is holding. You must work with someone you trust, like, and feel comfortable with. Trust your gut! It is not uncommon to go through a few therapists before settling on the right one.

How Much Trauma Healing Should You Do?

Everyone has different histories, so the amount of trauma healing that is beneficial will vary from person to person. It all depends on how many traumas you have experienced over your lifetime, and the severity of the trauma(s). An isolated traumatic event in your history may be quicker to heal than many traumas accumulated over a lifetime.

****

We have now covered trauma in this lifetime (whether it happened in infancy, childhood, adulthood, or some combination thereof), and how it can trigger overactive empathy.

There is one more place we need to look, however, to see if there are any further traumatic roots for overactive empathy, and this is in past lives.

When Overactive Empathy Has its Roots in a Past Life

I first noticed the link between overactive empathy and past lives when I began doing Akashic Record Readings for clients several years ago. As part of these readings, I would do some research into the past lives that had had a big impact on the client – for better or for worse.

Before I tell you about my discoveries in this area, I first want to give a more general introduction to how past lives can affect us.

How Past Lives Influence Us

Most of us have had at least one previous earthly incarnation – it is a rare soul who has not. And we can be influenced by our previous incarnations here. Past lives affect our likes, dislikes, strengths, fears, and even the kinds of situations we attract in our lives.

How This Works

How are past lives carried through into our present life?

There are a few mechanisms by which previous incarnations can affect us. One of the main ways is through past life sub-personalities.

What Is A Sub-Personality?

In psychology, a sub-personality is considered to be a fragment of one's self. We are all made up of many fragments. For example, in myself I am aware of the following sub-personalities: the perfectionist Anna, the Anna that loves to travel and have adventures, the Anna that is a homebody, the doting auntie, Anna the rebel, and Anna the nature lover.

All of these different parts of us have different needs and different thoughts about how we want to do things in our lives. Sometimes these thoughts are in harmony, and other times, they conflict, and we can 'be of two minds' about something.

These sub-personalities are a natural part of everyone's personality. However, in past life theory, we believe that some of these parts of us are influenced by or even originate from past lives.

This is often the case when we have been traumatised by something in a past life, and we make a promise to ourselves that this trauma will never happen to us again. The past life sub-personality then makes it their mission to keep us away from a similar situation in future lifetimes. Eventually that part of us begins to dominate, and even drives some of our choices and decisions. It steps forward and holds more sway over our actions, often causing us to over-compensate in our present life as a result.

I'm going to give you a couple of real-life examples of how sub-personalities can manifest and influence us, and how this encourages overactive empathy and sabotages empaths on the path to becoming more balanced.

Trigger warning: this next section contains some violent/traumatic stories from my own and others' past lives. Some readers may find them disturbing.

Failing to Help: Mary's Past Life

During a past life regression, Mary discovered a lifetime in a small village in Europe, several hundred years ago.

As part of that incarnation, Mary formed a 'past life complex' which involved guilt and self-punishment.

In that life, she was around age twelve when she came across a group of villagers who were taunting and tormenting an orphaned waif – a younger girl who was ragged, dirty and a stranger.

She knew the right thing was to step forward and defend this girl, but she didn't do it, because she was afraid that she would get the same treatment. She went home but could not forgive herself for not helping. This initiated a lifelong pattern of self-punishment – and to cope with this, she shut her heart down.

Because of this emotional shutdown, she became critical and harsh towards her own daughters. In particular, she was obsessed with making them obey the social rules of the village they lived in. She died in her fifties, still not having forgiven herself for this incident, and the ways she had behaved towards her own children.

This personality from Mary's past life was so intent on her avoiding this situation in future that it hung around and caused her to overcompensate in later incarnations. It influenced her choices. For Mary, this overcompensation in this lifetime involved helping others at her own expense, and by her own admission, behaving like a martyr in her personal relationships (especially with her children), tolerating abusive behaviours, and generally putting her own needs last in life.

The past life sub-personality that was influencing Mary is something that is commonly seen when one delves into past lives.

What is the link to overactive empathy here?

I have seen repeatedly through my work with clients that those who suffer from overactive empathy tend to be affected by one or more past life sub-personalities, and these sub-personalities are usually trying to protect us from making the same mistake we made in a previous lifetime. This 'mistake' was usually **a failure to help someone**, or a traumatic **incident where we blamed ourselves for something that was actually outside of our control**.

In short, empaths are often affected by past life complexes around **responsibility** and **guilt.**

Let's have a look at another example of how this pattern can play out for empaths.

Sandra's Past Life As a Healer

During a past life regression, Sandra discovered a past life in England during the Great Plague that was amplifying her empathic side. During that incarnation, she was the local healer, nurse, and midwife, and was deeply committed to her work, viewing it as her life's purpose.

METHODS FOR REDUCING OVERACTIVE EMPATHY

Sandra considered herself to be good at her job, until a plague arrived, and she became overwhelmed and exhausted by too many people falling sick. On top of that, her medicines and gifts were not effective against this new illness. She was surrounded by the dead, the dying and the terrified. She felt she ought to be able to help, but she couldn't do much. She too died of the plague during this epidemic.

The past life sub-personality that was Sandra in that lifetime was still stuck trying desperately to help, save and heal people. As a result, Sandra was being overly influenced by this past life character, and was still driven by the need to 'save' and heal others, no matter what the cost to herself. This resulted in Sandra finding it extremely hard to enforce boundaries with her children, clients and friends.

People would regularly take advantage of her, and she did not feel motivated to change anything about it, even though she was suffering because of it. This set up dynamics in Sandra's relationships which first triggered and then worsened her empathy.

****

A little further along in this chapter, I am going to cover **how we as empaths can resolve any past life complexes which we are carrying**, and which may be contributing to our overactive empathy.

Before I do, though, I would like to cover a second type of past life which is very common among empaths:

Empaths & Perpetrator Lifetimes

A perpetrator lifetime is one in which we work with dark energies, engaging in behaviours such as lying, manipulating, stealing, violating or hurting others in some other form. While we are experiencing this sort of lifetime, we are disconnected from the high vibration of our spirit.

While doing Akashic Record readings, I saw that empath clients who had 'unfinished business' from a perpetrator lifetime were more likely to self-sabotage on an unconscious level.

There are a lot of different ways in which this self-sabotage can manifest, but for empaths, I have seen time and again that these situations will often involve co-dependence, abusive relationships, and/or one-way relationships. And as discussed in the previous section, these types of relationships tend to heighten empathy.

So if you are someone who attracts unhealthy relationships, you will want to pay attention to this section, because perpetrator lifetimes are often a hidden factor in the question of why we attract these relationships in the first place, and why people struggle to break out of such dynamics.

Why Perpetrator Lifetimes Are Common Among Empaths

There is a very logical reason for perpetrator lifetimes to contribute to the development of empath gifts – this is because as souls, we seek wholeness and balance.

If I am poor in one lifetime, I often choose to be rich in the next. If I've been male in the last ten lifetimes, I will choose to be female for a while in the next ones. If I was ruthless, destructive or uncaring in my last life, I'll choose to care a great deal (as empaths do) in this one.

In this way, we get to experience ourselves as every facet of the Divine – the young and the old, the light and the dark, the male and the female, the rich and the poor, the hero and the anti-hero.

Why Souls Choose to Do This

I resonate strongly with something I read in the 'Conversations with God' series of books, which is that negativity exists because God wanted to experience relativity. The idea is that the Big Bang was effectively a shattering of God's energy into small particles (souls) so that God could experience Itself as many polar opposites – positive and negative, male and female, hot and cold, light and dark.

In seeing opposites, we get to experience negativity as well as positivity. Without the dark, there is no experience of light, and vice versa. In this process, we understand what we stand for on the soul level, and we ultimately come to identify ourselves as beings of love and light (which is indeed what we are).

This is exemplified in a lovely quote by the poet Kahlil Gibran:

"The deeper that sorrow carves into your being, the more joy you can contain.

Is not the cup that holds your wine the very cup that burned in the potter's oven?

And is not the lute that soothes your spirit, the very wood that was hollowed with knives?

When you are joyous, look deep into your heart and you shall find it is only that which has given you sorrow that is giving you joy.

When you are sorrowful look again in your heart, and you shall see that in truth you are weeping for that which has been your delight."

So, as souls we seek contrast - it is how we grow and evolve. So if you identify as an empath in this lifetime, it is likely that you will have had one or more previous incarnations as a perpetrator.

Next I want to tell you about my experience with perpetrator lifetimes, many of which cropped up for me during past life regressions, and also through dreams.

The Baby in the Lake

Throughout my life I had a recurring dream where I would discover human bones hidden in various places in my home, and I realised, in horror, that I was the one that had killed the person whose bones I kept finding.

Later, I became aware of a past life memory in which I had drowned my newborn baby as a young woman in a Southeast Asian country, and the shame I felt in the dream was the same distinct 'flavour' of shame that I experienced in the bone-finding dream.

In that lifetime, I was living with a man who had left to fight a war in the winter time. There was a famine and I found myself alone with no one to provide for us, so I fully expected to die of starvation. I gave birth to my child that winter, and instead of watching my child die of hunger, I decided to row out to the middle of a lake and drop her in.

In the regression, I discovered that I was suffering from post-natal depression, and I also went on to survive that famine. However, I carried a lot of guilt for the rest of my life that I had not given my child a chance to live, and that I was never punished for the killing – no one knew what I had done.

When discovering that lifetime, I also finally understood the nightmares I had had all my life about my loved ones drowning in a lake.

The Spanish Inquisitor

During another past life regression, I discovered a perpetrator lifetime that took place during the Spanish Inquisition. In that incarnation, I was totally dedicated to the teachings of the Catholic Church – I was quite the fundamentalist, and believed 100% in one God and one Truth.

I was involved in rubber stamping death warrants. Rather than seeking out evil things to do or being actively/physically involved in killing people or burning them at the stake, I was a bit more passive. I was mainly going along with a crazy system and set of beliefs, and I didn't have much compassion for 'heretics.' In that lifetime, I was emotionally blind and complacent.

The African Jailer

The third perpetrator lifetime I discovered during my past life regressions was as a warrior in West Africa. In that incarnation, I went from tribe to tribe with my gang, raping and pillaging. My role in the group was to do the bloody and cruel work that others couldn't bring themselves to do. (It was clear that I was a sadist and a psychopath in that lifetime).

In the latter half of that lifetime, I was kidnapped by the Portuguese as a slave, and became a jailer for them. As part of my role, I abused my power and killed many innocent souls in cold blood.

I believe that in a subtle but powerful way, releasing the guilt from these lifetimes finally liberated me from the self-punishment and self-sabotage that was causing me to choose unhealthy relationships, and indirectly contributing to my overactive empathy.

I am not the only one who has experienced this. Many of the empaths I have worked with have found that releasing one or more perpetrator lifetimes through past life regression has helped them to tone down their overactive empathy, and unlock more self love in an indirect way. This sort of work can help us to shift the dynamics of our relationships and the types of people we attract, which both have an impact on our empathy.

How to Identify Past Life Influences

So at this point, you may be wondering: "How can I find out if I am being affected by a past life sub-personality, or a perpetrator lifetime?"

As for perpetrator lifetimes, here are some signs you're being affected by this sort of past life influence:

- You feel unworthy and generally undeserving of the good things other people enjoy in life
- You have repetitive dreams where you're performing destructive deeds or being punished
- You regularly sacrifice yourself and your own needs, often engaging in co-dependent dynamics
- You feel a lot of resistance towards seeking out healthier dynamics in your relationships
- You struggle with shame

If you are very interested in or drawn to exploring your past lives, pay attention to that. The reason for this is usually because you have something to resolve there. Those who won't benefit from a past life work are usually not drawn to this type of healing at all.

How to Resolve the Past Life Influences That Commonly Affect Empaths

The most effective way to address negative past life influences is through past life regression, which utilises hypnosis to take you back to a previous life and relive what is still affecting you, with the aim of resolving it.

I have done about a dozen past life regression sessions (as a client), and I found them very helpful for accessing greater self love and self forgiveness, as well as overcoming overactive empathy.

I am also a trained past life regressionist and Akashic Record reader, who has seen similar results for my empath clients.

So if you are struggling to overcome your overactive empathy and bring it back into balance, and you suspect the reason for your overactive empathy goes deeper than this lifetime, you may benefit from past life regression healing.

How to Find A Good Past Life Regressionist

Not all past life regressionists are trained in helping people to release and heal perpetrator lifetimes. Some practitioners of past life regression will take you back to a lifetime, but don't give you an opportunity to heal it. This may be OK for exploring positive lifetimes (where we may connect with our good memories and anchor those in our current experience). However, it is not so effective for exploring difficult lifetimes.

In fact, if we explore our difficult past lives without healing them, what we are often doing is opening portals in the subconscious mind to the past events. This makes us even more aware of their influence in our lives, and they may leak into our dreams and inner lives with greater vividness and frequency than before. This is the exact opposite of what we want to achieve through past life work!

So if you are considering booking a session with a past life regressionist, I recommend that you enquire as to whether clearing and healing past lives will be a feature of the session. This is really important for empaths.

Next I want to cover another common influence in the development of empath gifts - namely, our family backgrounds.

The Relevance of the Ancestral Background in the Development of Empath Gifts

Similarly to past life traumas, the history of ancestors in our family can set the context for the activation of our empath gifts. In my experiences working with empaths, I have noticed that they are sometimes the grandchildren or great grandchildren of people who went through a great deal of trauma themselves.

This 'passing down of traumas' - or *intergenerational transmission of trauma* as it is known in psychology - can manifest as abuse or neglect (including emotionally distant parenting) in the family. As mentioned earlier in this chapter, both of those can lead to a person becoming an empath.

Not everyone who is traumatized will inflict their trauma on their children, but traumatized parents are more likely to trigger the activation of empath gifts in other ways, often without awareness of their actions.

I have heard many stories of traumas being passed down through the generations in my healing work, but in this next section I want to share with you my own ancestral background of traumas, and how they contributed to my development as an empath.

I am aware that not everyone will relate to this - my ancestral background is possibly more or less traumatic than yours, and some people do not know their family history.

My reason for sharing is to explain and illustrate the cycle of trauma that is referred to earlier on in this chapter, and hopefully get some of you thinking about your own family background, and how this may have contributed to your empathy.

My Grandparents & World War II

One of the ancestral contributors to my overactive empathy is that my grandparents had been traumatized. It is possible that the trauma started even before that, but I can only trace things as far back as my grandparents.

My maternal grandmother grew up near Liverpool, UK during World War II.

Liverpool was an important port city, and as a result, it was one of the places targeted by the German bombers. My grandmother spent many nights as a child hiding under the stairs in her family's rather inadequate bomb shelter. She experienced the trauma of hearing bombs being dropped, and explosions occurring. As she walked to school, she saw bombed-out neighbouring houses, and bodies blown apart by bombs still hanging from trees. And when she got to school she would sometimes find that her schoolmates were missing from their desks, never to return to school.

On top of this, shortly after the war ended, her beloved brother dropped dead one day at the age of ten in the local swimming baths – he had a heart defect that no one was aware of.

Around this time her mother contracted Multiple Sclerosis, and spent much of her time in a wheelchair. The impression I had of this period in my grandmother's life was that her mother was less available to her children emotionally and physically, and sadly, she died of the disease in her forties.

It became clear to me that little of my grandmother's grief or trauma was properly dealt with (the consciousness of that generation perhaps lacked the psychological and emotional awareness that subsequent generations benefited from), and so she unwittingly passed it on to the next generation.

Trauma is usually a factor in the development of personality disorders. Personality disordered parents then go on to cause trauma to their children, and so the cycle of trauma continues until someone breaks the chain. Abuse, personality disorders, addictions and abandonment were certainly themes in my childhood and adolescence as a direct result of my grandmother's issues. My grandparents were abusive and neglectful parents to my mother, who then parented my brothers and me in the same way. In addition, I spent a lot of time around my grandmother growing up, so I was influenced by her directly.

These traumas were not dealt with in my family, and led to the cycle of trauma continuing through the generations, which led to me becoming an empath.

****

I know I am not alone in this pattern. In working with my empath clients, I have found that many of them are the grandchildren and great-grandchildren of people who were traumatized in the First and Second World Wars. The Second World War in particular has been mentioned by many of my clients when they do the work of connecting the ancestral dots, and this does not surprise me. This war traumatized vast swathes of Western society: think about the bombing in many European cities, all the traumas experienced by soldiers in action, and of course, the devastation of the Holocaust.

I have seen through my work with empaths that there is a real connection here for empaths to World War II – not just an ancestral one but often a past life one, too. I personally believe it has set the context for many empaths who are struggling with their overactive empathy in the here and now, in many countries around the world. Yes, there has always been trauma in the world, but World War II was a traumatic event on a grand scale for many societies, and many of us are the children and grandchildren of those who were traumatised in this war.

So if you are someone who also became an empath due to circumstances within your family of origin, you may find further insight in researching or considering the events of your parents', grandparents', and even great-grandparents' lives. Considering your ancestral background is certainly not essential for bringing overactive empathy into balance, but it can be an interesting exercise for those who feel their upbringing made them empaths, and who want to explore this aspect further.

My Journey From Overwhelmed to Balanced Empath

At this point I want to give you a bit of background about my life and my story, so you can see the journey that I have been on, which has culminated in me writing this book, and helping other people with their overactive empathy.

How I Became An Empath

My story is probably a little different from most, in that I experienced most of the empath triggers listed in Chapter Two.

I was born in the UK in 1984 - one of five children, and the only girl. One of my parents has a personality disorder which made them emotionally unavailable and abusive.

As the only girl and a child of neglectful parents, I found myself in a care-taking role pretty early on. My younger brother (who was 18 months younger than me) did not speak until he was three and a half years old, so we developed a connection that bordered on telepathic. I knew what he wanted, and I was the one who got it for him. I believe this led to me being 'tuned in' to someone else's needs and energy from an early age.

Both of my parents (and my older brother) were physically and emotionally abusive. My older brother was later diagnosed with a personality disorder, and he made my life miserable between the ages of about 11-15. There were also other significantly traumatic events scattered in amongst the ongoing abuse.

During these traumas, I believe I went on little "trips" outside of my body, and this was most likely my introduction to the energetic/subtle realms that lay outside of ordinary human conscious awareness. I also became very good at 'reading' other people's energies and intentions to try to stay safe (essentially pre-empting what was going to happen next).

In hindsight, all of this was my initiation as an intuitive and an empath.

I continued my journey through adolescence as a deeply sensitive person. I became a perfectionistic over-achiever who suffered from low-self esteem. The only thing that could bolster my self-esteem was my academic success. I earned a place studying French & Spanish at university, and moved away from home.

Life in the Real World

Upon graduation from university, I moved to France and then to Spain to teach English. I had all kinds of cool experiences through my travels, and met some interesting people.

But I also really struggled during this time in my life. I had a series of unfulfilling and unhealthy relationships with men:

some of my partners were abusive, and others were simply emotionally unavailable. Romantic relationships seemed to be bad news for me.

At this time, my interests also shifted towards more spiritual matters, as I began to try to make sense of what I had experienced and where I was going. I sensed that I would not remain in the field of teaching languages for very long.

I became very interested in my past lives, and after getting an Akashic Record reading which told me about my life purpose, past lives, life lessons and gifts, I decided to train as a professional intuitive and Akashic Record reader.

In 2007, I started giving readings to others, and within several months I left my full time job as a languages teacher in Spain and moved to London to work for myself as an intuitive. I loved my new career, but it came with some unexpected downsides. My overactive empathy 'symptoms' began to worsen.

Opening up to other people's energies seemed to make me even more vulnerable to being energetically overwhelmed. Whatever negative energy was floating around out there in the subtle realm that is overlaid over our physical realm (such as other people's emotions, earthbound spirits, negative thoughts or bad energies left behind by awful events), I felt it.

Around this time, I became involved with another emotionally unavailable man, and I never knew where I stood. I felt anxious and hypervigilant trying to make sense of the mixed messages I often received in my relationship, which was a source of anguish. This connection somehow made my sensitivity worse.

And living in London, with its many people and energies, overwhelmed me.

It was at this time that I was guided to find resolution to the loose collection of symptoms that I now define as 'overactive empathy.'

Symptoms like:

- Feeling the world's pain and being unable to watch the news, or hear about what was going on in the world
- Withdrawing socially as a way to avoid other people's energies
- Experiencing difficulties in relationships because I could not stand to feel other people's negative emotions, and often felt responsible for resolving or helping them
- Putting my own needs last
- Being horribly drained by my work as a professional intuitive.

So trust me when I say I know what it is like to be overburdened as an empath.

Coming back into a state of balance was a journey that took me several years.

How It Happened...

First of all, I learned several important energy management tools (these are the techniques you have learned in Chapter One). I then started to teach these tools to my empath clients and students in our sessions together.

And secondly, I was aided in this task through my work as an intuitive healer, where I would release earthbound spirits and cut energetic cords for my clients. Most of the people who booked sessions with me were empaths.

They too often wanted guidance around how they could tone down their empath gifts, so they could feel less sensitive, less porous, and just less overwhelmed!

Working with these empaths, I started to channel guidance from the spirit realm around how they could come back into balance. My clients applied the new methods with success, and I also began to collect tips and pointers from Spirit on how overactive empathy could be brought back into balance, and applied them to my own life.

Through this process, I began to see the wider context of overactive empathy, and how many of the emotional and psychological issues that I was encountering in my life in my twenties were connected to this issue. I began to learn that the solution to the problem was not just a shielding exercise or a technique to release negative energies – it had to go deeper than that.

I also saw the same themes cropping up again and again, in my clients' lives and in their histories (and even their past lives). I noticed these same themes were reflected in my own history, too. And the more I actively worked on resolving them, the more my empath gifts came back into balance, and the less energetically overwhelmed I felt.

This has shown me that as overwhelmed empaths, we need to understand the role that our unique history and background has played in making us who we are.

And so to bring ourselves back into balance, and remain there, we need to keep in mind the following:

Being an overwhelmed empath is not about having a gift that is divorced from all the other aspects of your life or your history. It is a logical outcome of your background, your soul's past and path, and all the things that have happened to you in your life to this point.

Coming back into balance is about identifying and working on those triggers in your life, and from your past, that may be pushing you into energetic overwhelm, so that you can embrace your soul's true path, learn the lessons you're meant to learn, and contribute your amazing empath gifts to the world.

Chapter Two, Part Three
The Emotional Projection Trap

We are moving towards the end of this chapter, but before we finish, I want to cover one more possible cause of energetic overwhelm for emotional empaths – what I call the **"emotional projection trap."**

This may apply to you if you are an emotional empath who has already spent some time exploring the solutions given in Chapter Two of this book, but still struggles with overactive empathy. Experience has shown me that this is a common trap for my emotional empath clients to fall into. I explain what it is in the examples below.

****

Gemma's Grief

My client Gemma (an emotional empath) was attending the funeral of someone she didn't know – her partner's boss' wife. Even though she had never actually met this person and knew little about her, Gemma felt overwhelmed by grief during the ceremony, and sobbed all the way through it.

What was the reason for this?

Was Gemma picking up on the grief of the mourners around her?

Quite possibly, yes – but when I did a reading for Gemma, I picked up that she was **mistaking her own emotions for those of other people.**

When we dug a little deeper, she told me that her brother's wife Louise (who was also her good friend) died in a car accident one year earlier - a loss she felt she had not grieved, as she was about to give birth to her first child and was doing her best to support her brother. She remembers feeling devastated, but successfully holding in her emotions at the funeral – a very different experience from the outpouring of grief that came over her at the funeral of someone she barely knew.

This kind of emotional projection is something many empaths engage in, and it is something I have also done myself: I describe two of my own experiences with this phenomenon below.

Amy Winehouse

When the singer Amy Winehouse died from alcohol intoxication in 2010, I was completely devastated, and mourned the loss for weeks. Although I enjoyed her music, I was not the world's biggest Amy Winehouse fan, so the emotions I was feeling appeared to be disproportionate.

At first, I thought I was feeling the world's grief around her death. But I realized later that what I was really mourning was the loss of one of my own parents to alcoholism. I also suspect that as an empath, I may also have been picking up on other people's grief around Amy's death. But in retrospect, I can see that a lot of this grief was actually mine, and was simply misplaced and unresolved.

Losing My Cat

There was another clear occurrence of this phenomenon in my life, shortly after my beloved pet cat had an embolism and dropped dead one night in front of me on the living room floor.

A few months after his death, I was out driving when I saw a big, ginger cat go under the wheels of a truck. Another woman and I stopped our cars on the side of the road to try and help. The woman scooped up the injured cat, handed him to me, and asked me to come to the vet with her. I got into the back seat of her car, and she drove to the vet, which was just around the corner. Sadly, the cat died on the way there.

This experience hit me very hard. The cat didn't have a microchip, and so there was no way for the vet to figure out who the animal belonged to. I knew I had to go and find the cat's owner, though, to let her know what had happened, so I went knocking on doors near where the cat had had the accident. And just when I was about to give up, I came upon a woman outside her house, calling for her missing pet. I told her what had happened, described the cat, and she confirmed it was hers.

This event set off an outpouring of grief for me, and it wasn't until much later that I realised was probably crying more than, or as much as, for my own cat than I was for hers.

****

A decade of experience working with empaths has shown me that this scenario is very common - essentially, emotional empaths who are suppressing their own negative emotions will often get triggered when they go into settings or have experiences that involve bumping up against other people's strong negative emotions. This effectively gives the empath a chance to release those strong feelings.

Looking back, it now seems totally obvious to me that the experience of seeing a cat dying would have triggered a lot of grief for me. But the fact is, when we are feeling these strong emotions, we don't always have the clarity to see what is really going on. And as empaths we sometimes just assume that what we are feeling must be someone else's. After all, our emotional lives can get so clouded by our empath gifts - because we feel so much anyway, it can all get a bit confusing!

Around the time that I heard about Gemma's experience, something else occurred in my own life that highlighted just how much emotional repression was taking place for me.

Chronic Pain & Emotional Repression

In 2012, I developed a **chronic pain condition** called RSI (repetitive strain injury) that affected my hands, arms and wrists. I was no longer able to write, type, cook, drive, clean, lift, or work with my clients.

Over a period of a few months, I went to see a physiotherapist, an acupuncturist, a massage therapist, and did strength training and stretching to help my muscles. The consensus among these therapists was that I had RSI because I was working too much, and not keeping my muscles strong or stretching them enough. Rest was recommended.

Although I was fortunate to be able to keep my business running during this time (as I learned to control my computer with my voice), I was concerned because I had heard personal accounts from people who had had this condition for many years, and there seemed to be few who had healed it successfully.

After about five months of suffering with this condition, however, I stumbled upon the cure. Bear with me while I tell you what it was, and explain what I believe is the relevance of this to us as emotional empaths!

Healing the Pain

I came upon the solution to my chronic pain when my massage therapist sent me a book by a Dr. John Sarno.

Dr. John Sarno (1923-2017) was an American physician who noticed that many of his patients with unexplained chronic pain conditions appeared to have certain personality traits in common. Over time, he came to believe that most instances of chronic pain — including back pain, gastrointestinal disorders, migraines and fibromyalgia — are physical manifestations of **suppressed emotions in the unconscious mind** (primarily rage, frustration and grief).

Sarno posited that the human unconscious mind has evolved to consider strong negative emotions as threatening to our survival, and is prone to creating physical pain in the body in order to distract us from these emotions. This is achieved by cutting off a little bit of the oxygen blood supply to a certain area of the body (in my case the hands and arms) - not enough to cause any damage, but just enough to cause some pain. Sarno also believed that a cure could be found by becoming aware of and expressing these repressed emotions.

Although Sarno's theories remained controversial in the medical community, he developed a solid reputation among his patients for successfully treating intractable chronic pain conditions, and was lauded by celebrities such as Howard Stern and Larry David.

Does Sarno's theory sound a bit far-fetched to you? Well, I was skeptical, too.

I put his book away for a while, but then a curious coincidence occurred. The person I had just hired to cook for me (as I was no longer able to do this for myself) spotted the book on my shelf, and told me that she had recently overcome many years of chronic back pain by using Dr. Sarno's methods. Prior to this, she had spent many years bed-ridden and unable to move around.

My cook's testimony motivated me to try out the Sarno method for my pain. This involved three steps:

- Daily journaling and reflecting on all the challenging things in my life - past and present
- Dialoguing with my body to let it know that I wanted it to stop distracting me from my emotional pain

- Tuning in to how I really felt on a daily basis

And to my surprise, it worked – it felt like a miracle. However, although the 'cure' was pretty much instant, I did relapse frequently over the months that followed, and I had to tune back in to my unconscious mind and feel what was there. It was not an enjoyable process as I dredged up repressed grief, sadness, frustration, fear and rage and felt it, like my life depended on it.

It was a healing journey that resulted in me feeling much lighter emotionally from having released and processed so many emotions, and also feeling much more connected to my emotions.

So, these days when I get pain in my hands, I know I have something I need to face up to, emotionally speaking, and I am able to resolve the pain when it does crop up.

So why did I tell you this long story about my recovery from chronic pain?

Well, an interesting side effect of this journey is that as an emotional empath, I noticed I was feeling other people's emotions less, once I started to feel my own more often. I had less cause to use the clearing techniques in Chapter One, because I was absorbing less emotional debris from the people around me. I was no longer stuck in a painful, never-ending cycle of attracting what I myself was actually carrying on an emotional level.

So here is what my guides, and those of my clients, have often reminded us – I want to repeat it here because it is an important lesson for those of us who do avoid our emotions:

It is healthy and normal as a human being to feel a range of negative emotions. People may not often talk about their negative feelings to one another, but as someone who has been privy to the inner lives of plenty of people (as a cord cutting therapist and intuitive reader) – almost everyone feels these feelings. They are universal.

We are here to experience duality and contrast – the positive and the negative – and to evolve as a result. It is part of the conditions here on earth. And part of experiencing the positives and the negatives means having an emotional aspect that we get to grapple with.

But many struggle with our emotions because we live in a society that encourages us to be emotionally shut down. I believe there is an evolutionary aspect to this, in that the world has historically been (and still remains to some extent) a place where we will at times encounter injustice, and where it hasn't always been safe to be closely acquainted with one's feelings of anger or frustration.

Anger in particular compels us to act, and taking action might not always be in our best interests (at least from the point of view of the ancient part of our mind that is primarily concerned with survival, and considers it wisest to keep our heads down and say/do nothing)!

On top of this, some of us grow up in families that encourage emotional repression. If you grew up with a narcissistic, addicted, or emotionally unavailable parent, this probably applies to you. Personally, I was raised in an emotionally constipated family, and was often given the message that it was not okay for me to feel the way I did. In fact, I wasn't conscious at all of what I was feeling a lot of the time. I realized that my sixth sense had heightened itself from childhood, to compensate for what I had been missing emotionally.

It isn't just personality disordered, addicted or emotionally unavailable parents who raise children in a backdrop of emotional repression, though. Empath parents may do this, too. For example, I remember hearing about a friend who went out into the woods with her children, when they were burying their pet rabbit who had recently died.

My friend's little boy (who was about seven years old) started to cry, but she instructed him not to grieve anymore over his beloved pet. My friend was not comfortable with her child's pain (a difficult thing for all empathic parents) in that moment, and so the little boy repressed the natural process of catharsis that would have helped him to release the sadness of losing his bunny.

But by repressing our emotions, as empaths we are actually prolonging our emotional discomfort or pain, because when we avoid our negative emotions, we experience and attract more of whatever emotion (anger, sadness, anxiety) that we are repressing in ourselves. And as a result, **we may find ourselves in a painful cycle of attracting the same**

emotional gunk over and over, until we reconnect with what we are really feeling.

This is one obvious negative consequence to emotional repression. But there is another: by repressing our emotions, we lose out on what those emotions may be telling us about our lives.

THE MEANING OF NEGATIVE EMOTIONS

All of the darker, heavier emotions that show up for us **are actually giving us feedback about our lives and our desires.** Thus when we are repressing our emotional aspects, we miss out on the important feedback these feelings are giving us about our lives:

- **Anger** helps us to set boundaries, and to protect and stand up for ourselves
- **Sadness** helps us to relax and let go of the old, so that we can create room for new experiences
- **Grief** helps to heal ourselves, and integrate life changes following a loss
- **Fear** can keep us away from genuine dangers, and prompts us to seek security and comfort in our lives
- **Jealousy** or **envy** may point us towards what it is we are lacking, and what we wish to create or manifest for ourselves. It may also prompt us to look at our blessings, and practise gratitude for what we do have.
- **Guilt** compels us to make amends, learn from our mistakes, and take responsibility for our actions

- **Shame** encourages us to accept ourselves (and others) as we are, flaws and all

When we repress the messages that these useful emotions bring to us, we are more prone to remaining stuck, or even getting ourselves into dangerous or unwanted situations.

Next I am going to tell you a story from my past which is a clear example of this principle in action (it was not my finest hour, so please do not judge too harshly)!

Ignoring My Anger

Part of my journey reconnecting with my emotions has been about becoming aware of my feelings of anger, and allowing them to guide me and keep me safe. This is something I failed to do for myself in my twenties, when I careened from one appalling relationship to another (often with men who were narcissistic or abusive.)

I had one boyfriend (let's call him Markus) who was psychologically and verbally abusive.

He would (among other lovely behaviours) gaslight me, put me down, humiliate me in public, give me the silent treatment, mock me, call me names, and throw things at me. We weren't together for long, but this treatment went on for weeks, and I remember that it felt pretty awful at the time.

All of this behaviour made me angry. However, at the time I believed that anger was not an appropriate response to have – I was conditioned to feel that way because I grew up in an abusive and dysfunctional family, and as a child I was not able to respond in a self-protective way. As a result, I had not yet learned how to stand up for myself.

Markus exploited this situation, and encouraged me to think that any anger I felt was unjustified and not his problem. He also kept telling me that we were meant to be together, because I was a healer and needed to help him heal his problems. He made me feel sorry for him, and as a result I put up with him for longer than I should have.

Then one day when I was walking down a street in the centre of London with Markus, he tripped me up on purpose (for his own amusement) on a packed pavement next to a busy road. I lost it - I got up off the ground and hit him hard in the face, twice.

I thought to myself, "How did we end up here, with me on the pavement and him getting smacked in the face on a busy London street? What in the hell are we doing?"

Picking Myself Up Off The Floor

The answer to that was that I was being treated badly and lashing out because I had swallowed my anger for weeks (and indeed for years). I ended our relationship soon after that incident, but it took a couple more bad relationships and a few more years to learn my lesson and finally get in touch with my anger - to start seeing it for the genuine gift it was.

Stored Up Grief & Sadness

It is not just the repression of anger that can cause problems in our lives - unprocessed grief can also wreak havoc on our health and our hearts.

Grief is of course what we experience in scenarios where we lose something that is important to us - it might be the loss of a loved one, a beloved pet, a job, a home, or even the death of a dream.

But grief is another emotion that our Western society is not all that comfortable with, and that we are encouraged to repress. I believe the main reason for this is that we don't like to watch one another suffer, or witness our loved ones do the painful 'heavy lifting' of grief work that allows them to process a loss. All we see is their pain, because we are less familiar with the liberation and wholeness that comes once the grieving is over and a new chapter opens up.

There is a brilliant book about grief called *Tear Soup* that I often recommend to grieving clients.

This book uses soup making as a metaphor for grieving, and in the story, we follow an elderly lady, Grandy, in her 'soup making' (aka. grieving) after a loss. We see her rejecting the idea of glossing over her loss and getting over it as quickly as possible (i.e. taking a tin of soup off the shelf because it is quicker)!

Instead, she goes through the difficult process of 'making soup' from scratch. She cries many tears, eats a lot of comfort food, remembers the good and the bad times, meets up with a support group where they all eat soup together, and visits a good friend who helps her make bread to go with the soup. She slows down, connects with what she is feeling, and does the work of processing and remembering.

Eventually, she puts the rest of the soup away in the freezer, knowing that occasionally she may take a little out to taste it again.

By contrast to this process, when we 'take a tin of soup off the shelf' (i.e. put a sticking plaster over our hearts and carry on without properly processing what has happened), this can prolong our grief. Unprocessed grief does not go away - it waits for the time when it will be recognised for what it is, and tended to appropriately. It reminds us of its presence in a variety of ways, often manifesting somatically (in the body) in the form of physical ailments - i.e. insomnia, gastrointestinal issues, headaches, and muscular pain. It can also cause or contribute towards depression, addictions, compulsive behaviours, chronic fatigue, and overactive empathy.

I hope that by this point I have convinced you of the importance of practising awareness of your own heavy emotions as an empath. So if you are an emotional empath who sees yourself in the descriptions above, you may be wondering how you can connect more with your emotional aspect.

Next I want to go into a few tips and pointers on how we as empaths can accomplish this.

How to Reconnect With Stored Up Negative Emotion

If you are an emotional empath who feels a lot of other people's negative emotions, it is always a good idea to have a process where you regularly 'tune in' and connect with your feelings. Below you will find a few exercises to help with this.

1. Journalling to Release Negative Emotions

Journalling is an excellent way to become aware of, and express your feelings. When you journal, you can express anything you like, no matter how intense or negative, and you are the only one who needs to read it.

Below you will find the exercise Dr. John Sarno recommended for recovering from chronic pain. My work with emotional empaths has taught me that it is equally useful for recovering from overactive empathy (at least wherever emotional projections/repression are contributing to this).

It is as follows:

Write about the things that have caused you stress, anger or pain in your life – present or past. Consider the questions below. Please note that not all of them may apply to you.

- What are the life events or situations, past and present that have caused stress for you?
- How do you feel right now, in this moment?
- Who are you angry with/what are you angry about?
- What fears do you have?

If you're doing this for the first time, go over your past and think about all the misfortunes you've had, the pain and sorrow you've endured in your life, and the difficulties you've overcome. Hold nothing back, and really consider the impact that all these things have had on you. This is your space to wallow and feel sorry for yourself (if necessary).

If you're doing this exercise on an ongoing basis, you will want to use it much like journalling, where you check in with yourself and feel whatever it is you're feeling at the moment, with a focus on the negative stuff. Talk to yourself about anything challenging that is going on in your life, and have a moan about it.

Here is a question my clients have asked me about this process in the past:

"But won't I attract more of the bad stuff or get depressed if I focus on the challenges in my past and present?"

On the contrary – what we resist, persists. When we as empaths become aware of our negative emotions and allow them to flow through us, more peace, love, and contentment becomes available to us. Catharsis is the name of the game!

By contrast, if we fail to process our own negative emotions, we are more likely as empaths to feel too much of the negative emotions of those around us.

Secondly, if you have any concerns about focusing too much on the negative aspects of your life, counteract this exercise with a positive one, by journalling about what you are grateful for in your life. Personally, I like to follow up journalling about my worries and stresses with a gratitude list.

The above exercise can easily be underestimated, because it seems like a very simple one, but doing this on a regular basis is so very powerful for empaths who feel too much of other people's emotional 'stuff'.

Now let's have a look at the next exercise for emotional expression and release.

2. Release Anger

Anger is another intense emotion that generally requires some degree of expression in order for us to remain in good health. Anger can scare some people, mainly because we may associate being angry with raised voices, verbal abuse, or even physical violence. Some people prefer to avoid conflict, because it can be unpleasant!

However, there are wiser ways to be guided by our anger…and then release it.

The Purpose of Anger

As mentioned earlier, the purpose of anger is to helps us to set boundaries, and to protect and stand up for ourselves.

Often our anger is telling us that something is wrong, and that we need to speak up about it or take some other action. For example, your partner made a hurtful comment and you're still annoyed about it. Your anger is telling you that you need to talk to him/her about it and get it straightened out, and perhaps he/she needs to apologise. If this is something that happens on a daily basis, maybe you need to take a different kind of action. There are many possibilities here, and your anger, if you allow yourself to feel it, can help show you which solution might be the right one.

Some people worry that if they take action or speak based on their anger, this may spoil their relationships. But people who damage their relationships because they have anger management problems are not typically empaths. In my work with empaths, it is clear that on the whole, they are fairly compassionate people who give others the benefit of the doubt, and tend to forgive easily. If they get angry about something, it is usually because they have a good reason to.

Thus, speaking up and expressing ourselves is one way to deal with our anger and let it guide us.

But let's face it, it is not possible to do this in every situation, because we do live in an unjust world. We don't always have the opportunity to take action or speak up about the things which have personally made us angry.

As a result, sometimes other methods are needed to help process our anger. I have shared my favourite strategies below, in case anyone finds them helpful.

Just a note that the methods I mention below might sound like basic common sense, but in my experience we don't actually process or release our anger as much as we could, because we are not socialised to do so (especially women).

As a cord cutting practitioner, I have found that when I tune in to clients' chakra systems, one of the most common energies that I tend to find hanging out in people's (especially women's) throat chakras is **anger**. We often don't realise we are storing it, and again we may trigger some of our own stored up anger when we find ourselves face to face with other people's injustices.

So how can we release this heavy emotion?

Hitting Inanimate Objects

Hitting things (rather than people!) is an excellent release for anger – this may consist of beating pillows or using a punchbag. When I was grieving the loss of one of my parents, I was also very angry, and I used to punch a pillow to deal with that emotion. I also went to boxing lessons, which were extremely cathartic. An exercise such as this allows us to release our angry impulses without hurting anyone, or ourselves.

I was also gifted crockery by someone who had angered me. I decided I didn't want it anymore, and so I went out into the back yard and threw it all against the brick wall! It made a hell of a mess, but it really helped me to let go.

Listening to Angry Music

Another of my favourite ways to release anger is to listen to angry music. I have a few go-to songs which I like to crank up, and an 'angry' playlist on YouTube.

A few of my favourite angry songs are 'You Oughta Know' and 'All I Really Want' by Alanis Morissette, 'Bad Blood' by Taylor Swift, 'Survivor' by Destiny's Child, and 'Zombie' by the Cranberries.

****

A Summary of Chapter Two & Further Tips for the Healing Path

- If you suffer from overactive empathy, most likely you are either being **invited to take inventory of the health of your relationships, or you're being prompted to heal or release something** about your past (if you do not resonate with either of these explanations, you may wish to check out Appendix E at the end of this book…)

- **Stay open and curious when exploring what issues might be at the root of your overactive empathy.** Use your intuition. The trigger for your overactive empathy could be one factor, or it could be a combination of many. The more open-minded you can be to the possibilities, the easier it is to identify and resolve your personal triggers.

- **By identifying your triggers and following the methods and pointers presented in this chapter, it is possible to bring your empathy back into balance.** Bear in mind, however, that healing can take time and energy to do – it is not a process that necessarily occurs overnight, so be patient and gentle with yourself.

- **Recovery from trauma in particular is not usually something that is ever 100% complete,** as it tends to be an ongoing process throughout a person's life. This does not mean that you need to be 100% healed to bring your empath gifts back into balance - you may just need to heal enough to reach the tipping point for you personally.

- **Once you have brought your empath gifts back into balance, you will find it much easier to integrate your empath gifts into your life in a positive way,** and actually benefit from them in your life. In the next chapter, we will look at how to develop practices and habits which enable you to live your best life as an empath!

Chapter Three

Making The Most Of Your Empath Gifts

Have you ever felt that your life would be a whole lot easier if you could just erase the sensitive part of your temperament and become more like a non-empath?

From working with my sensitive clients and students, I have noticed that this is a sentiment expressed by many of them – we empaths can get into the habit of observing our less energetically porous peers and 'comparing our insides with other people's outsides' (as the saying goes). We may come to the conclusion that we would have it easier in this world if we weren't so darned sensitive. And as a result, we may wish this part of our temperament away.

On top of that, the people in our lives can sometimes fail to value our sensitive side – many of the empaths I have worked with have, as children, been shamed by their family or teachers for being "too sensitive." Then in later life, they may feel misunderstood in their relationships with non-empaths (bearing in mind that only 8-10% of the population are sensitive in this way).

But the problem with wishing away our empath gifts is that **empathy is usually an integral part of our soul's purpose.**

So in this section, I am going to dive deeper into this link between soul purpose and our empath gifts.

I am also going to talk about how we can honour our high level of empathy and bring it into the world more fully - a world that doesn't always value these gifts outwardly, but one that needs them nonetheless.

By the time you have reached the end of this section, I hope you will be persuaded that your empath gifts are invaluable and beautiful gifts that enrich your life and the lives of others!

Our Soul Purpose As Empaths

So let's start by unpacking the statement I made earlier: "**our sensitivity as empaths is usually an integral part of our soul's purpose.**"

The Empath's Place In The World

As you have probably noticed by now, incarnating on planet Earth isn't necessarily a walk in the park.

Although we can have all kinds of wonderful experiences on the physical plane, it is not always a harmonious, kind or gentle place to be.

The reason for this is that this particular place of incarnation (Earth) is one where souls can evolve through contrasts, and the biggest contrast of all may be the one between positive and negative (or light and dark).

As souls, we are here to explore themes like love, truth, power, peace, security, joy, freedom, faith and wholeness. But we can also very effectively learn about these energies by coming into contact with their opposites - victimhood instead of power, hatred or indifference instead of love, suffering instead of joy, and constraint rather than freedom. By experiencing those negative energies, we are more able to fully understand their opposites.

In a creative writing class that I took several years ago, I was taught that it is the presence of the villain in a story which drives the plot forward, making it interesting. It is harder to define and explore the hero of the story, unless there is an anti-hero or a villain for the hero to struggle against. Without the dark, we cannot get to know the light. And in my experience as an Akashic Record reader, that's quite an apt metaphor for how soul evolution operates on earth.

To offer one example that has come up for a few of my clients, souls who are here to learn a primary life lesson of self-love will sometimes incarnate into an abusive family in order to learn this lesson. By choosing an abusive parent who does not model love or self-care, the client ends up experiencing the pain that comes from a lack of self-love. She internalises the abuse, and often develops a critical inner voice that results from how she was raised.

But in adulthood, she may go to work on eliminating that critical inner voice. Perhaps she did not receive much mothering, and thus she has to learn to be her own mother, and learn how to love herself. By living without the energy of love from her parents, she is motivated to explore that energy more fully in her own self and life, so that she can heal and move forward.

We can of course also explore self-love by having a wonderful childhood experience with parents who model and embody the energy of love. But my work as an Akashic Record reader has shown me that some souls opt to experience the negative side of a contrast in order to learn, because this is actually a very fast and effective way to explore a life lesson.

The World's A Stage

*"All the world's a stage,
And all the men and women merely players"*
   -Shakespeare, 'As You Like It'

As souls, we all have a part to play in the exploration of these negative and positive energies, for ourselves and for others. As empaths, we are here to bring positive energies into the world, and to counterbalance those souls who are here in a perpetrator lifetime to sow discord. They tend to see no one's side of the story but their own, and bring destructive energies into the world, such as abuse, cruelty, division, insensitivity, oppression, and fear.

We play our part by bringing the energies of **understanding, harmony, cooperation, healing** and **love** into the physical.

So as a group, we are for the most part encouraging others to live in harmony, helping people to heal, caring for others, emphasizing doing the 'right thing,' and loving people.

How Do We Do This?

You may have heard the saying that "you are the product of the five people with whom you spend the most time." It is true that we all influence one another unconsciously – I'm sure you have had the experience of spending a lot of time with a very negative person who complains a lot. If you spend enough time with such an individual, you'll usually find yourself beginning to take on such behaviours and mentalities. This is the effect of coming into contact with someone's aura on a regular basis.

This is how we bring our energies to other souls – all people teach one another through their presence on earth. So we don't just bring the energies of understanding, harmony, cooperation, healing, sensitivity and love into the physical. We also encourage other souls to integrate those energies further into their own being and into their own lives – we are a force for good on this planet. And what is more, this is something that we often do not need to 'try' or plan to do – instead, it is something that often happens naturally for us in our everyday lives.

This is not to imply that empaths do not have a shadow side, because like everyone on this planet, they do. When empaths are out of integrity, they can deceive themselves and others, engage in manipulation, and hurt people. However, in my experience working with empaths, I have seen that they generally care deeply about the impact they have on other people.

How Can Empaths Bring Their Positive Energies More Fully Into The World?

I mentioned above that we bring certain positive energies into the physical, often without trying. But what if we want to embrace our empath gifts, and be more active in bringing them into the world?

Something Spirit has told me in readings with empaths is that by consciously choosing daily activities which allow us to use our empath gifts, we can access greater fulfilment and increase self-esteem.

Finding Activities That Use Your Amazing Empath Gifts

Below is a list of careers and activities which can make use of your empath gifts:

Activities/Careers Which Utilise Empath Gifts

- Healing of all kinds, including physical, emotional, spiritual, and psychological healing. Empaths may choose to train as doctors, dentists, veterinarians, acupuncturists, Reiki practitioners, massage therapists, psychotherapists, Craniosacral therapists, or herbalists, to name just a few.

- Psychic or spiritual work, such as intuitive reading, life/spiritual coaching or spiritual counselling
- Artistic and creative professions or activities, where the focus is on creating beautiful things, such as paintings, sculptures, or graphic design
- Acting and performing, which require inhabiting characters and expressing emotional experiences with the psychological nuances and emotional insight to which the empath is already attuned
- Professional care taking, such as nursing, caring for senior citizens, child minding, nannying and pet sitting
- Marketing and business – in these professions, empaths are able to use their empathy to gain insights into what customers need and want, and how products and services may be presented in a way that appeals to potential customers
- Writing fiction or non-fiction; editing and translating. These tasks involve understanding or expressing the finer nuances of the human psyche and soul, and bringing these to life in a written text.
- Mediating and conflict resolution (or any peacekeeping role, formal or informal, where one gets to see a situation from another person's point of view, and take that person's needs or stance into account)
- Teaching – emotional empaths are better able to relate to the learning challenges experienced by their students. Psychological empaths usually have an affinity for other

people's learning methods and thought processes, and thus they also make excellent teachers.

- Any profession which involves beautifying or improving the look and feel of a space (place empaths are particularly good at this, as they are sensitive to the energy of environments). This may include feng shui consulting, interior designing, or gardening (especially for plant empaths).

- Parenting: being sensitive is an advantageous trait for a parent to have. Empath parents have a greater ability to empathise and relate to their children and their experiences. Children who feel emotionally validated tend to grow up into emotionally healthy adults.

This does not mean that empaths need to switch careers (unless they are already guided in that direction). We can also express our gifts further by simply incorporating some of the above activities into our everyday lives. For example, an empath may find fulfilment in taking a Reiki class and giving Reiki treatments in her spare time. Or she may volunteer as a teacher, or spend more time with the children in her family.

How Are You Already Using Your Empath Gifts?

When reading the list above, take note of the ways in which you might currently be using your empath gifts in your work, your spare time, or your personal relationships. This may help to illustrate the positive impact your sensitive temperament (and the skills linked to it) may have had in your life - and in other people's lives - thus far.

As for me, although I am currently using my empath gifts as a businessperson, writer, intuitive and healer, I was using them long before I got into the field of metaphysics and healing in 2007.

At University, I trained in foreign languages (not an uncommon degree choice for an empath, I've noticed). I excelled in written translations, and I felt that my sensitivity gave me an edge in this pursuit - after all, empaths often experience things energetically, and thus gain experience in 'translating' the energies they feel, and putting words to them. I felt that this energetically sensitive, intuitive part of my brain came into play during my translation exercises.

At the time of writing, I am also a professional house sitter (looking after people's homes and pets while they are out of town or overseas).

To find house sitting work, I have a house sitting profile on a website that emphasises my high attunement to, and empathy for animals. Some of the home owners who have approached me to house sit for them, told me they did so because they felt I would be sensitive to the needs of their animal(s). I've often been asked to look after timid or abused rescue pets who need a gentle approach.

How Might You Further Use Your Empath Abilities In Your Life?

If you are someone who wants to use their gifts in their everyday life, you might like to do a brainstorm for ideas to bring your sensitive self more fully into your work, relationships or leisure time.

Jot down any ideas you have below.

_____

_____

_____

_____

_____

_____

_____

AVOIDING SITUATIONS & PEOPLE WHO DO NOT VALUE OUR GIFTS

Let's have a look at the second suggestion for empaths to make the most of who we are: steering clear of people and activities that do not honour our gifts. This is quite simple – it usually involves paying attention to the intuitive signals which tell you when you are surrounding yourself with people who do not value your sensitive nature. The result of this is usually a lack of fulfilment, feelings of inadequacy, and receiving little or no credit for your contributions.

I have several experiences with this, as do some of my past clients.

Next I am going to tell you a story about a time in my early twenties when I got into just such a situation.

Finding the Right Career As A Sensitive Soul

When I graduated from University, I had no absolutely idea what I was going to do with the rest of my life, career wise.

I knew I was good at foreign languages, but I didn't want to be a translator (because although I was good at it, I felt it was also boring and repetitive work). Nor did I want to be teaching French and Spanish to high school children.

I went to a University with a lot of high fliers who had successfully found jobs in the civil service and in the corporate world, working in areas like management consulting, investment banking, and recruitment. So initially in my job search, I just copied what everyone else was doing.

I was very much unsuited for the types of jobs I was applying for, but I didn't know it yet. I recall one interview process that was particularly torturous:

The day of the interview, I made my way into inner city London wearing my power suit. Going into the big city got my hackles up before I even got there - I am not a city person at all!

During the interview, I discovered that I was to be put in a room with the other candidates, and we had to interview each other and sniff out who was NOT suited for the position we had all applied for. I was soon outed as the weakest link, as the other candidates commented on my lack of skills in selling myself or anything else, and my shy and uncompetitive nature at the time. During the interview I felt like a gazelle with a pack of lions circling around me – the whole process was so uncomfortable that I wanted to walk out mid-interview and leave that place behind!

It was clear I was wholly unsuited to the job, which required a lot of self-confidence, a 'me-first' attitude, and a very competitive spirit.

I left that day feeling completely demoralised – why couldn't I sell myself or anything else? Why was I not a persuasive oral communicator? Why did I feel uncomfortable poking holes in the other candidates or trying to sniff out their weaknesses? And lastly, why couldn't I think on my feet as quickly as I needed to?

I felt bad about myself. But now I know that failing at that interview was a good thing, because I wasn't passionate about any of those jobs, nor was I suited to them. I would not have lasted two minutes in the corporate world – I was simply emulating my peers and going through the motions, hoping it would all fall into place somehow.

I had a temperament that was very different from the people who successfully interviewed for that job, because they were undoubtedly more suited to the corporate world, and I was more suited for starting my own business in the field of healing and metaphysics.

Now I wish I could have told Anna of 2005 that she was going to make a successful and fulfilling career from writing and teaching in the fields of intuition and healing. I also would have told her that she was a non-conformist empath, and that it was OK to be gentle as a person. She also didn't need to be extroverted to succeed, and certainly not competitive or aggressive.

We need to remind ourselves as empaths that there is a positive place for us in society – a place where our gifts and contributions are valued. Sometimes it does not feel this way, because Western societies typically reward and value ambition, competitiveness, and the ruthless pursuit of profit – all of which come more easily to those who have a thick skin and a disregard for the needs of others. For this reason, people who lack empathy are disproportionately represented in leadership positions, in the corporate world and in the banking industry.

As an aside, I did a Google search for the words: 'psychopaths' and 'success'. I found countless online articles on the topic, including a recent Australian study[1], which found that as many as 1 in 5 CEOs are psychopaths.

Mind you, I am not saying that all of those people I interviewed with were psychopaths. What I am saying is that the corporate and work culture in Western society is one which rewards those with psychopathic traits, and so those people with these traits (i.e. no scruples or a lack of empathy for other people) can often achieve success in the corporate world more quickly and effectively than those without such traits.

---

1   Nathan Brooks & Katarina Fritzon, 'Psychopathic Personality Characteristics Amongst High Functioning Populations' (Crime Psychology Review, 2016)

So what's an empath to do? Is it a case of 'nice guys always finish last?' Had we better toughen up and act more like non-empaths if we want to get ahead in life?

No! My experience (and that of my clients) is that empaths can be highly successful & self-actualized by being their authentic selves, but there are some caveats:

We must choose the right field or industry for us. I know that personally I do not have the right temperament to be a successful banker, a civil servant, or an accountant, for example.

I am more suited to being a self-employed healer, an intuitive, a teacher and a writer, where I use my sensitivity to pick up information for my clients and relate to the learning challenges of my students. I do well in roles where I can nurture and support people and their spiritual growth.

Similarly, many of my empath clients are using their gifts in roles such as coaching, intuitive counselling, healing, writing, creative work, and parenting.

So as empaths, we can succeed too, but we must do so through means that are better suited to our sensitive natures. We perform well in roles where we are bringing insight and creativity into the world, taking the needs of the community into account, or where we are tuned into the needs and feelings of other people.

When have you put yourself forward for situations or relationships that did not honour your sensitive side?

It might be helpful to consider times in the past when this has happened in your life. What kind of intuitive signals (if any) did you receive at the time?

Jot down any ideas below.

_____
_____
_____
_____
_____
_____
_____

Using Our Empath Superpowers to Read People

As empaths, we might sometimes feel like it's only other people who get to benefit from our empath gifts, but it doesn't have to be that way! Did you know that as an empath, you have talents that allow you to read people for their intentions, personality, and more? Once you have learned how to control your gifts, you can benefit from them yourself in this way, and have some fun in the process.

In this chapter, I'm going to share a technique for finding out about a individual's character, intentions and levels of integrity - all without even needing to meet with, or even speak to the individual in question.

This method is helpful for both personal and professional relationships, and preferably used before the relationship really gets underway. I say this because once you get to know somebody, it becomes harder to be objective in reading him or her.

This approach is also especially useful for hiring staff - choosing babysitters or home help, for example. I use this technique when hiring staff for my business. Obviously it is not the only vetting step I have in place as a businessperson, but it is one more useful way to really find out about another person, while cutting past all of the facades that other people present to the world.

Occasionally, out of interest and curiosity, I also use this method if someone in the public eye intrigues me, and I want to find out who they really are underneath everything that they project to the general public. This might be a politician I am considering voting for, or someone who is accused of murder in a controversial case.

When I do this, I am aware that I cannot know for sure if the person committed the murder or not. When I tune in, I do not have a spirit popping up telling me all about what happened. Instead, I research the person's inner life - what they are feeling and experiencing (or not feeling, by contrast).

I research a variety of different chakras, which paint a clear picture of what is REALLY going on with that person at the moment, and within their true character. I am able to establish whether their inner life and character are consistent with having murdered someone or not – I will get a definite sense either way, but I won't know 100% for sure.

It's a fascinating exercise. Occasionally my findings appear to be wildly different from the way the person comes across on the surface, or the way they are portrayed in court or by the media.

How This Method Uses Your Empath Gifts

The technique I am going to teach you actually propels you inside someone else's experience, so that you feel what it is like to be him or her from the inside, rather than observing the subject's energy from the outside. It will give you a vivid experience of what life is like for the person you are reading.

I believe that all empaths can benefit from using the techniques taught in this section. The reason for this is because narcissists, bullies and sociopaths are often drawn to empaths, and it is up to us to be selective about who we let into our lives. Oftentimes a person's actions and words do tell us what we need to know about him/her, but this approach can give us an additional layer of information or confirmation regarding our impressions about that person.

The method I am going to teach you does rely on a certain degree of familiarity with the chakra system, so let's have a quick look at what that is, in case there is anyone reading who is not familiar with it.

The Chakra System

As mentioned earlier on in this book, there are layers of energy (known as the subtle energy bodies) around the physical human body. These energy bodies (among them the mental, emotional, etheric, and spiritual bodies) together make up the aura. The energy in the aura is centered around seven main hubs called 'chakras.'

A chakra is an energy centre that receives life force energy from the Divine. Each chakra receives a different type of energy, such as communication or personal power energy - all of which are necessary for life here on earth. This energy is then integrated and expressed in the person's life, so the chakras contain information about a person's soul, strengths, lessons, past, and present.

The ways in which one integrates and expresses these chakra energies can be observed from the inside out when an empath tunes into a person's chakras.

For those of you do not have a basic familiarity with the chakra system, please read the following information about it below:

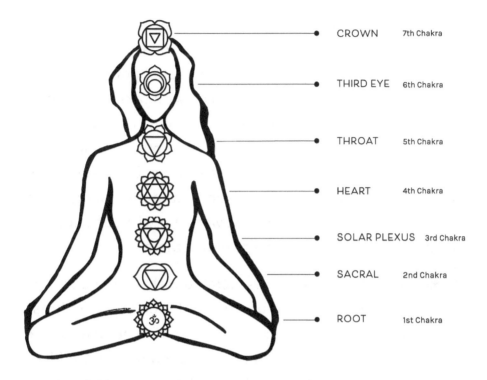

CROWN	7th Chakra
THIRD EYE	6th Chakra
THROAT	5th Chakra
HEART	4th Chakra
SOLAR PLEXUS	3rd Chakra
SACRAL	2nd Chakra
ROOT	1st Chakra

The Root Chakra (red) is located at the perineum. It is the chakra that represents our foundation and connection to the world, and all the material things in it. It represents physical safety and material security, being most concerned with our survival in this world. It also represents money and the financial part of life. If we fear for our financial security or feel unsafe in the world, it will show up at this chakra.

The Sacral Chakra (orange) is located just below the belly button. This is the chakra of pleasure, creativity, abundance, sensuality, sexuality and the emotions. The physical pleasures of life are experienced at this chakra. If we have any hang-ups about sexuality or inhibitions regarding enjoyment of life, it will show up here.

The Solar Plexus Chakra (yellow) is located just above the belly button. It is associated with our personal power in interactions with other people, and our personal power to make things happen in our lives. It has to do with taking our ideas and acting on them by using self-discipline and willpower. It is also where we assert ourselves and our boundaries. A well-balanced solar plexus means that we can assert our boundaries and create what we want, without pushing other people around or abusing our power, and without allowing ourselves to be taken advantage of by others.

The Heart Chakra (green) is associated with love, and serves as the bridge between the upper and lower three chakras. Centred at this chakra is our relationship with ourselves. The heart chakra is like a fountain or a cup – the more we fill it up with self-nurturing and self-loving energies, the more we can share those vibrations with others. On the other hand, if we neglect ourselves and sacrifice our desires in order to please other people, this will show up at the heart chakra, and our loving relationships will be more challenging as a result, because the loving energies that are usually present at the heart chakra will be depleted. As a result, we will be 'running on empty,' emotionally speaking, and may feel resentful when giving to others.

The Throat Chakra (blue) is associated with self-expression and communication. This is where we ask for what we want or need, and speak our personal truths. This is also where we hear other people's truths. If we have hang-ups regarding self-expression, this will show up at the throat chakra.

The Third-Eye Chakra (lilac) is located between the eyebrows. Centred here at the third eye are our powers of clairvoyance, which literally means 'clear-seeing' – it is our ability to see the world clearly. This chakra is where we perceive the truth, and use our intuition to get clarity and go straight to the heart of the matter. It is also where we focus our intent to visualize and create what we want in our lives.

The Crown Chakra (white) is located just above the head in the image shown above. This chakra is at the opposite end of the spectrum from the root chakra – while the root chakra is associated with our day-to-day physical life, the crown chakra is concerned with our spiritual experiences.

Centred at this chakra is our connection to our Higher Selves and our Spirit Guides. If we have had negative experiences in a religious setting that still affect us, these will often be stored at the crown chakra. If for some reason we are cut off from Spirit, it will also be visible at this chakra. Ideally the crown chakra will be connected fully with Source energy.

How to Read a Person's Chakras

To be able to do this type of reading for someone, you can visualise him/her clearly in your mind's eye (which is like the movie screen you see in your mind when you close your eyes).

If you cannot easily visualise the person you would like to read, you will need to find a picture of the person in question.

Here are some requirements for obtaining a photo:

- There should only be one person in the photo
- Make sure you can see the person's eyes clearly, and that the photo is not too small
- It should be a recent photo (meaning one from the last couple of years)

Now that you have a suitable photo in front of you, here are the steps for the reading:

1. Choose an Ascended Master/Archangel to bring in for this reading. (If you wish to be reminded of the Ascended Masters and Archangels that we can bring in for this exercise, please see page 50 of this book.)

   Once you have chosen your Ascended Master/Archangel, here is how to call in that being for this exercise:

   - Say **Archangel Michael** (or whichever Divine energy you have chosen), **please be with me.**
   - Do the following breathing exercises: inhale to the count of four, hold to the count of four, and exhale to the count of eight. Do this a total of three times.
   - Now it is time to prepare your space energetically for the reading so that you are less likely to be affected by the energies you encounter during the reading:

2. Ask for violet flames and white light for the room you are in. The violet flames are a receptacle for cleared negative energies, and the white light is to protect your space.

Archangel Michael (or the Divine-level energy you personally called in for this), **please place violet flames in every corner of this room for transmuting negative energies.**

Please also place your white light of protection around the edges of this room, so that only high vibrational energies may enter.

I ask for a temple of love, light and truth to be anchored through me now and I send my root chakra energy to the core of mother Earth, to ground me.

Creating An Energy Dome

The next step is to create an 'energy dome' for reading the other person. Here is how to do this:

1. Close your eyes. Visualize the person you're reading sitting opposite you at a table - if you're already sitting at a table or desk, you may wish to visualize the person sitting opposite you.

2. Now imagine taking their hands from across the table and holding each hand in yours. This connects you to their energy.

3. Next, see a golden light just above your crown chakra (over your head). See this light turn into a large 'dome' that is directly above you. It grows downward and envelops you and the person you're reading in golden light. Now you both have a golden curtain of energy around you on all sides, and you are enclosed in this space with the person

you're reading. If you prefer, you can also imagine putting up a tent around you both to create that space.

Now you are going to experience what that person is like, by reading his or her chakras.

The Root Chakra - Body

Say **Archangel Michael, give me insights into _____'s physical experience.**

You can say this out loud or in your mind.

Take a deep breath. Write down anything you notice.

Here are some questions you can ask to get more detail:

- How safe does this person feel?
- Has she got a good grip on reality, or does she feel 'far away?'
- How connected is she to her physical experience and body?

For this exercise, feel free to close your eyes or breathe deeply. Everything that happens in your body, emotions, or mind upon asking the above questions counts as information for this exercise.

The Sacral Chakra - Vitality & Creativity

Say **Archangel Michael, give me insights into _____'s sense of creativity and vitality.**

Take a deep breath. Write down anything you notice.

Here are some questions you can ask to get more detail:

- How vital and 'alive' does this person feel?
- How much does she enjoy life?
- How creative is she?

THE SOLAR PLEXUS CHAKRA - POWER

Next, explore the person's sense of power in the world.

Say **Archangel Michael, give me insights into_____'s sense of power in the world.**

Take a deep breath. Write down anything you notice.

Here are some questions you can ask to get more detail:

- How effective is this person in the world – is she able to get things done and achieve what she wants to?
- How does she share power in relationships?
- How self-confident is she?

THE HEART CHAKRA - EMOTIONS

Say **Archangel Michael, give me insights into _____'s heart.**

Take a deep breath. Write down anything you notice.

You may also ask more specific questions in this area, such as:

- Does this person feel connected to her loved ones?
- Is she good at giving, or receiving, or both?
- What is her style in caring for and loving people?
- Does this person really care about other people?

Make notes on what you notice and experience when you ask these questions.

THE THROAT CHAKRA - SELF-EXPRESSION

Next, explore their self-expression. Focus on their throat chakra (at their neck).

Say **Archangel Michael, give me insights into _____'s sense of self-expression.**

Take a deep breath. Write down anything you notice.

Here is a question you can ask to glean more detail:

- Is this person able to confidently speak her truth?

THE THIRD EYE CHAKRA - INTELLECT

Next, explore the client's mental energy. Focus on their third eye chakra (between your eyebrows).

Say **Archangel Michael, give me insights into _____'s mind.**

Take a deep breath. Write down anything you notice.

Here are some questions you can ask to get more detail:

- What is this person's mental/intellectual energy like at the moment (i.e. scattered, focused, clear, etc.)?
- How far under the surface of reality is she able to see? Is she very intuitive?
- How does she see herself?

The Crown Chakra - Spirituality

Now you can explore the person's spirituality. Focus on their crown chakra (above their head).

Say **Archangel Michael, give me insights into _____'s spiritual life.**

Take a deep breath. Write down anything you notice.

Here is a question you can ask to get more detail:

- Does this person have a relationship with anything she considers a 'higher power,' such as God, Spirit, or Source?

By putting your impression together, you can paint a picture of who this person is.

How to Interpret the Information

Sometimes we may pick up information during an exercise such as this one, but without knowing how to interpret it.

For example, when tuning into someone's third eye chakra, perhaps you pick up a sense of power or strength. You know that the third eye chakra is the centre of the **intellect, imagination** and **intuition**. So what does this impression refer to or mean?

In order to find out, you will need to ask!

Tell your intuition to show you what the impression refers to. If you know how to dowse using a pendulum, you could ask your pendulum to show you whether the impression is in reference to the person's intuition, intellect or imagination (with yes/no answers). Perhaps by doing this, you infer that the person is of high intelligence and is a thinker.

Negative Energies

Sometimes, we empaths pick up on struggles that a person is having when we read a person's chakras. For example, you sense that perhaps the person you are reading has a lot of repressed energy at the throat chakra. You sense that this causes some discomfort and frustration for him, and that it manifests as him being reserved in relationships and unable to express his feelings.

Sometimes empaths also pick up on earthbound spirits, negative thought forms, unwanted influencing energies, and other types of 'energy clutter.'

If you get a feeling, like a creepy, dark or eerie feeling when reading someone, ask your intuition why – and attempt to get some clarity around it. What does it relate to? There is always another layer of information, and more clarity and specificity to be had.

Sometimes you need to be in a meditative state in order to get that extra information - doing deep breathing will put you there.

Your empath gifts on their own will give you a basic sense as to whether you like or trust someone or not. In order to receive more details, you need to use your other clair senses. So if you pick up on 'a bad feeling', dig a bit deeper and see if you can work out why you feel that way.

After This Exercise

Since you have used your empathy to read another person, make sure you cut psychic ties afterwards, as per the exercise in Chapter One!

Chapter Four
Advanced Energetic Protection for Healers & Intuitives

I have noticed that many of my empath clients practise alternative healing modalities and do intuitive readings for others, whether professionally or as amateurs. So this chapter has been designed for those empaths who want some advanced tools for energy protection and management to use in their client sessions.

The techniques provided in Chapter One for clearing out astral energies such as psychic ties and emotional residues are definitely helpful in this kind of setting, and I recommend all empaths use those two protocols when working with clients. But there are a few additional tools and practices which I personally use as an empathic intuitive/healer – they work well to prevent me from taking on negative energies from my clients, so that I feel more balanced and grounded after a session rather than drained, hyperactive, or uncentered.

Let's have a look at the first advanced tool in the empath practitioner's toolkit:

Tool #1: Bringing Divine Energy Into Your Sessions

In Chapter One, we learned how to work with Archangels and Ascended Masters to clear out negative astral-level energies from our auric fields. These Divine-level beings are not just helpful for **clearing out** negative energies – they can actually **protect us** from negative energies during our client sessions, too.

They do this by enabling us to position ourselves vibrationally at the Divine level (rather than the astral level) during a session. In this way, we take a bit of the Divine into every session, and more easily avoid taking on astral-level debris (such as earthbound spirits and emotional residues) in the process.

In addition, when we bring Ascended Masters or Archangels into our client sessions (whether it be a healing or intuitive session), we are also creating an environment that is restorative, gentle and loving, making our sessions a more enjoyable and sacred experience for everyone involved.

Below are the steps for bringing Divine energy into your client sessions:

1. First, choose an Ascended Master or an Archangel (I usually select Archangel Michael, but feel free to choose anyone you like) to accompany you for your client session.
2. Then, say: **Archangel Michael** (or whichever being you have chosen for your session), *please be with me.*

3. Next, do the following breathing exercise: inhale to the count of four, hold your breath to the count of four, then exhale to the count of eight. Do this three times in total. The presence of the Divine energy will now be with you.

4. If you are doing an intuitive reading, you may also wish to say the following:

Dear Divine Presence, I surrender this session to you. I ask for the grace to be a clear channel for guidance. I ask for the grace to listen and speak from a wise, heart-centred place. I ask for my Divine team to work with the Divine team of (client's name) *in a high vibration session for the highest good of all concerned. Thank you.*

Now let's have a look at the second step for protecting your energy during a healing session or a reading: setting up violet flames.

Tool #2: Setting up Violet Flames

Why Set Up Violet Flames?

When you work with clients as a healer or an intuitive reader, you will come into contact with many energies. Often these energies can be heavy or negative (especially if you are working as a healer). Violet flames stop you from being affected by clients' negative experiences and emotions during a session. The flames neutralize any negative energies for us, so that we don't process these energies (consciously or subconsciously) on behalf of the client, or allow them to adversely affect us. Instead, we remain neutral observers.

So here is the prayer to set up violet flames before client sessions:

Archangel Michael (or whichever Divine energy you want to call upon), **I ask that you fill and surround me and** (client's name) **with your violet flame for the duration of this session, transforming any fears, concerns, and worries into love, faith and serenity.**

Archangel Michael, I ask that you fill and surround my space (and _____'s space) **with your violet flame, removing and neutralising any negative energy, and raising the energy in these places to a high vibration of love.**

Thank you.

Now let's look at the third tool we can use for energetic protection as an intuitive or healer.

Tool #3: Setting Up White Light

After you have requested violet flames, you may also wish to request a white light of protection for your space and for your energy field. This prayer protects the energy in your space for the duration of the session.

Here is a prayer that will enable you to do this:

Archangel Michael, please place your white light of protection around the edges of my home, so that only high vibrational energies may enter. Please also place this light of protection around my energy field. Thank you.

Now on to the fourth advanced energetic protection tool for practitioners...

Tool #4: Having a Spiritual 'Logging off' Process

I call this a 'logging off' process because I personally like to think of the spirit world as being a bit like the internet! You can access so much information and connect with many beings, which is wonderful. But you do not want to be logged on to the internet (i.e. in a state of energetic openness) all day long, getting distracting notifications about other people or events. You want to 'log off' so you can return to your day, and focus on what is important in your own life.

Therefore, if you do not already have a set 'logging off' process for completing your client sessions, I recommend that you create one! I have included mine below.

How to Energetically Complete an Intuitive or Healing Session

1. When you reach the end of the session, thank the Ascended Master/Archangel you brought in during the first step.

   For example:

   Thank you Archangel Michael for bringing the healing energy of this session (if it was a healing) OR **Thank you Archangel Michael for being in charge of this session** (if it was a reading).

2. Next, cut all psychic ties and connections between you and the client by saying the following:

   Archangel Michael (or whichever being you called in), **I ask you to clear all psychic ties that may have formed between me and _____. Please dissolve all these ties with a beam of gold light, in every dimension, through time and space. Please fill me and _____ with the energies of love, truth, light and power. Thank you.**

3. Next, remove any emotional residues from your energy field:

   Archangel Michael (or whichever Divine energy you have chosen), **remove from my energy field any suffering, fear, anxiety, anger, shame, discomfort or any other negative emotional energies that do not belong to me.**

   Remove from my aura anything that is not my burden to carry.

   Remove from my aura anything that is not my burden to carry.

   Remove from my aura anything that is not my burden to carry.

   Cleanse my aura of all this energy now.

4. Next, close off your energy field:

   I call on Archangel Michael to fill and surround me with Divine Love, Divine Truth, and Divine Light. Please close off my energy field to all except my Higher Self and those beings of the highest consciousness, who are meant to be with me on my spiritual path.

5. Then say the following:

I am now back in my body. This session is complete.

This statement signals to the Ascended Master/Archangel/Spirit Guides who have helped you that you are finished with the session. It basically communicates to all involved that energetically the session is over.

When Do You Say These Prayers?

When I was offering client sessions, I said these prayers once I had hung up the phone with the client. Some people also choose to say them on the phone or in person with the client, at the end of the session.

Now let's have a look at the fifth and final tool for energy management when working with clients…

Tool #5: Keeping Good Boundaries

Boundaries are very important for empathic intuitives and healers. By boundaries in this context, I mean avoiding taking responsibility or ownership of issues or problems that belong to your clients. It also means having a clear idea of what you are able and willing to do for your clients, and what you are not available for.

The reason why boundaries are of particular importance for empathic intuitives and healers is because our boundaries in the real world actually have an impact on our energetic well-being. If your boundaries with your clients are flimsy or poorly defined, this will affect the integrity of your own energy field.

Tips for Keeping Good Boundaries with Clients

1. **Plan how much time you will spend on a session**

   Before the session begins, make sure you set some expectations around how long the client can expect it to last. If the session is intended to last for one hour, do not let it last an hour and a half or two hours – routinely going over time when you do not intend to, and the client has not paid you to, is a drain on your energy field. It can weaken your solar plexus chakra, which is your power center.

   If you find yourself routinely going over time with clients, you may need to reassess what you offer and how much you charge. For example, if you offer a 60-minute session and keep going over time, why not offer a 75-minute session and charge extra for it?

   Some practitioners struggle with charging enough for their sessions. Sometimes we come across potential clients who feel that because what we do is spiritual, it should be offered for free. I've found this attitude can come most often from spiritualists, who have traditionally done readings as a hobby, and have requested a gold coin donation for their services at spiritualist meetings.

2. **Decide how available you want to be outside of sessions, and stick to it**

   This mainly applies to intuitive readers, as it is not uncommon for clients to come back and request more insight following a reading, and it is sometimes unclear whether this work falls under the category of what has already been paid for, or whether the client should book another session.

If you are someone who offers follow-up questions for your sessions, you may need to let clients know how many of these questions (if any) you are available to answer, and for how long the client may send their questions.

Personally, I have a 'no follow-up questions' policy, stating the following on my sessions page:

"Please make sure you get all your important issues and questions addressed during the session, as I am not able to answer questions outside of phone sessions due to time constraints."

I know of readers who feel they have to take multiple follow-up 'clarifying questions' for their readings (even months after the original reading was delivered), because they have not set limits on the scope of what is actually offered in the reading. I also used to do this.

However, we must be careful that we are not opening ourselves up to being a never-ending pit of time and energy for our clients. There is always going to be the odd client who tries to get more than their money's worth, and may take advantage of the empath's good nature. These are the type of people who will send multiple follow-up questions long after the reading is completed, rather than book another reading. It is up to us as practitioners to set some boundaries around our time, and ask our clients to schedule another reading or session for their follow-up questions (if indeed we even offer that).

3. **Screen clients for drama**

   Sometimes clients book a session because they are going through some kind of crisis in their lives.

   The following statements in an initial communication with a potential client are red flags that this client might turn out to be triggering for you as an empath:

   "I need a session this afternoon" (and the client complains or gets pushy if you are unable/unwilling to put them in the calendar straight away).

   "I'm in crisis."

   "You're the only one who can help me – you're my last chance."

   To avoid working with clients who are in crisis or in a place in their lives where they may bring a lot of drama into your practice, it's a good idea to have a statement such as the following on your 'sessions' or 'terms of service' page:

   "My sessions are not a substitute for advice or treatment that you would normally receive from a professional such as a lawyer, doctor, psychiatrist, or financial advisor."

   I also add the following:

   "All sessions are for personal growth and spiritual purposes."

* *

That concludes this chapter.

If you work with clients in a professional capacity as an intuitive or healer. I hope that you found the tips in this section helpful!

Intuitive and healing work really are a beautiful use of the empath's gifts, so the more tools we have at our disposal to keep us feeling balanced and energetically clear during our client sessions, the more people we can help, and the more we are able to enjoy our work!

Happy healing/reading!

Summary of the Protocol I Use For Beginning & Ending Client Sessions

I wanted to provide this document as a resource for your client sessions, so that you have all the steps I use for beginning and ending sessions at a glance.

Beginning A Session

1. Bring In An Ascended Master/Archangel For Your Client Session

1. First, choose a Divine-level energy (I usually choose Archangel Michael, but feel free to choose anyone you like) to accompany you for your client session.
2. Then, say: **Archangel Michael** (or whichever being you have chosen for your session) **please be with me.**

3. Next do the following breathing exercise: inhale to the count of four, hold your breath to the count of four, then exhale to the count of eight. Do this three times in total. The presence of the Divine energy will now be with you.

4. If you are doing an intuitive reading, you may also wish to say the following:

Dear Divine Presence, I surrender this session to you. I ask for the grace to be a clear channel for guidance. I ask for the grace to listen and speak from a wise, heart-centred place. I ask for my Divine team to work with the Divine team of (client's name) **in a high vibration session for the highest good of all concerned. Thank you, thank you, thank you.**

2. Set Up A Violet Flame

Archangel Michael (or whichever Divine-level energy you want to call on), **I ask that you fill and surround me and** (client's name) **with your violet flame for the duration of this session, transforming any fears, concerns and worries, into love, faith and serenity.**

Archangel Michael, I ask that you fill and surround my space (and _____'s space) **with your violet flame, removing and neutralising any negative energy, and raising the energy in these places to a high vibration of love.**

Thank you, thank you, thank you.

3. Set Up a White Light Of Protection

Archangel Michael, please place your white light of protection around the edges of my home, so that only high vibrational energies may enter. Please also place this light of protection around my energy field. Thank you.

Ending A Session

4. Thank the Divine Energy

Thank you Archangel Michael for bringing the healing energy of this session (if it was a healing) OR *Thank you Archangel Michael for being in charge of this session* (if it was a reading).

5. Cut Psychic Ties

Archangel Michael (or whichever being you called in), *I ask you to clear all psychic ties that may have formed between me and _____. Please dissolve all these ties with a beam of gold light, in every dimension, through time and space. Please fill me and _____ with the energies of love, truth, light and power. Thank you.*

6. Remove Emotional Residues

Archangel Michael (or whichever Divine energy you have chosen), *remove from my energy field any suffering, fear, anxiety, anger, shame, discomfort or any other negative emotional energies that do not belong to me.*

Remove from my aura anything that is not my burden to carry.

Remove from my aura anything that is not my burden to carry.

Remove from my aura anything that is not my burden to carry.

Cleanse my aura of all this energy now.

7. Close Off Your Aura

I call on Archangel Michael to fill and surround me with Divine Love, Divine Truth, and Divine Light. Please close off my energy field to all beings except my Higher Self and those beings of the highest consciousness, who are meant to be with me on my spiritual path.

8. Complete The Session

I am now back in my body. This session is complete.

Conclusion

When I was going through my journey of overcoming overactive empathy, and researching content written for empaths (there wasn't as much of it available back then). Much of the material aimed at empaths recommended steps like:

- Shielding techniques (i.e. visualising an energetic shield around you)
- Using crystals to protect yourself
- Tips on how to have better boundaries and become more assertive with difficult or demanding people in your life

It took some time and experimenting for me to realise that these solutions were probably effective for balanced empaths, but only a temporary sticking plaster for truly overwhelmed empaths.

Then rather serendipitously, life took me on a journey to find the best solutions for me personally. And the gratifying part about finding my solutions was that they appeared to help other overwhelmed empaths too.

Below is some feedback from a former student and reader of this book:

"I just wanted to give you some feedback in regards to the "Empath's Toolkit" I read last year. It has been a thoroughly eye opening experience and unbelievably helpful to me. It has explained so much about the weird and unexplainable symptoms/feelings I experience daily. Since I do not have any empaths around me to tell me what is going on, I needed this book. It has helped to end the suffering of thinking I was losing my mind. Also the medical community called me a hypochondriac because I have so many symptoms that change from one day to the next. I now know that some of it was physical and emotional empathy. It is the awareness that is the true gift.

This book opened my eyes to how much trauma I was carrying, and didn't know it. I put myself into therapy this summer to help heal from PTSD. I found a lovely woman who specializes in Somatic Experiencing. At first, my anxiety increased and stayed quite uncomfortable for 6 months. But, it is starting to decrease now as I am gaining tools to calm myself and also releasing traumas. Through therapy, I learned I was taking on other people's emotions because I did not want to feel my own feelings. I joined an additional group for people with PTSD. In this group, we are asked to feel how another person might feel. My therapist feels I was doing that all the time. She called it "Doubling".

I still get overwhelmed in crowds, but it is more manageable now because I understand what is going on!" - Suzanne Flynn, Lords Valley, PA.

Takeaways

The message I hope that **overwhelmed empaths** will take away from this book is that all the boundaries, lifestyle adjustments, and shielding visualisations in the world will not make much difference to your overactive empathy in the long term, if you don't also consider the root causes.

With some work and some time, these causes can be addressed and overactive empathy overcome. This is not an overnight process, and it isn't always easy, but it does work.

However, the issue must be addressed from the inside out - not the outside in!

Here's a quick summary of the points covered in this book:

- As an empath, you will be picking up on other people's energies on a daily basis. Therefore, it is a good idea to use energy clearing techniques regularly to help remove these influences
- Our early childhood experiences and relationships can set us up to become empaths in the first place
- Whether we are a balanced empath or an overwhelmed empath (or somewhere in between) depends on what happens to us as we go through life. It also depends upon the people we choose to have in our lives, and how those people treat us
- We can bring overactive empathy back into balance by *releasing* past traumas, and there are many modalities and therapists out there that can help with this

- We may also bring overactive empathy back into balance by changing unhealthy/toxic dynamics in our relationships - or where possible, releasing any toxic connections that cannot be changed

- Not all empaths have been affected by trauma, but many have been at some point (see Appendix E for more on this.)

- Many emotional empaths have a tendency to be out of touch with their emotions, projecting them outward onto other people. To avoid picking up on these energies in your environment, try to release and process your own stored up negative emotions through journalling

- Past life regression can a helpful healing modality to try if you have a hard time setting boundaries or looking out for your own interests

- Our empath gifts are part of our souls' purpose here - we must value them!

- Empaths are here to be of service if they so choose, but they are not here to suffer, put themselves last, be martyrs, co-dependents or doormats

I wish you all the best on your journey. If you wish to be part of a community on your path of empath healing or exploration, come visit me at AnnaSayce.com.

Appendix A

Protecting Oneself From Negative Media

In this section, I want to pass on some further recommendations, tips and essays on overactive empathy which do not fit into any of the other chapters. I am going to begin with my thoughts on empaths' relationship to modern media.

To Follow Or Not to Follow The News?

Many empaths have a difficult relationship with the media (news websites, TV, radio, etc.), simply because they are so sensitive to other people's energies.

Deciding whether or not to follow the news can certainly be difficult if you are an empath and you feel like you need/want to stay informed. The choice for empaths seems to be, do you try to shut down your heart and 'toughen up' while reading about the news? Or do you avoid it altogether and end up feeling uninformed or disconnected from what is going on in the world?

I believe there is a middle path to be found here…

Personally, ever since I was little I have shed tears for people I have seen on the television, or read about in the news, and

I have a huge capacity to feel pain that is not mine. It's been called neurotic, too emotional, or oversensitive. It's actually the intuitive gift of empathy, expressed in a particularly unhelpful way.

It's unhelpful because being plugged into others emotionally on a global scale is useless, unless you plan to do something practical about it.

On the other hand, in a tribal context, emotional empathy and sensitivity were actually wonderful evolutionary mechanisms that have helped human beings for a long time – we need empaths within a community. They are able to anticipate feelings and help keep the peace. They are (and have been) the mediators who can see and feel both sides of a story. They are often the ones that lend an ear and a shoulder to others in times of disappointment and sadness. They are able to validate the emotional and spiritual experiences of others.

So, in a tribal or community context, empathy makes sense, because it can be followed through with action.

Plugged Into the Whole World?

Now this evolutionary advantage of sensitivity and empathy has the potential to weaken us – emotionally and mentally – in the new era of information. These days, we're not just plugged into our own families and our communities, we're also able to be plugged into the citizens of countries we've never been to and know little about. We can read about bad things that have happened to these people. We are able to see and vicariously experience their difficult experiences on our television screens.

In no period of history have we as empaths ever been so exposed to the pain and problems of so many.

But For What?

Unless you plan to help poverty-stricken or suffering people in practical ways, what is the point of reading and watching such news?

No one (and that includes empaths) can help the whole world, unless they decide to have a career on the international stage. I believe that empathy works best in a one-to-one context, and as such, empaths are usually here to bring their gifts to those closest to them – their family, community and the people they work with.

There are 7.5 billion people in the world, and a lot of things happen to those people in any given day. Some of these things are good, and some are bad. Yet most international news sites seem to be a run-down of the most atrocious, tragic, gory, unfair and awful things to happen to the most unfortunate on our planet.

If you feel what others feel easily, it's madness to be plugged into it every day. I have come to the conclusion that being exposed to such a horrid and tragic selection of what goes on in the world on a daily basis is downright toxic for the empath's mind and heart.

The Answer – Being in Touch with Reality Without Hurting Ourselves

As mentioned earlier, I believe there is a middle path to be found here:

Some spiritual and sensitive people do avoid negativity and even bury their heads in the sand when it comes to what goes on in the world. I know I have done that at times.

But I don't think it is necessary to disconnect completely from everything that is difficult about this world and pretend that it doesn't exist, that we've transcended it, or are okay with it. And it is not necessary to let the spirit of activism die.

Personally, my mantra is: I will plug in if I am in a position to help.

If I can't help you or offer support in some way that honours both of us, I won't plug in to you and feel what you're dealing with, because otherwise I'm wasting my time and my energy.

It doesn't mean I lose compassion for you - it's just that I don't lose my emotional energy over it.

Empathy and sensitivity are gifts to be honoured and protected. They make you function differently from some people. But that doesn't mean you need to do as most people do. Most people don't have the same level of sensitivity as you (if you are reading this). So don't allow modern media and the information connection with the entire world to swallow up your emotional energy and leave you exhausted.

Empaths have always been, and continue to be, most useful in their own backyards.

So when something awful does occur in the world, simply ask yourself, what can I do about it? Can I pray for those affected? Can I help in some other practical way?

Once you have done what you want or feel able to do, move on and live your life as much as you can. If you feel overwhelmed by grief, hand it over to God/the Universe (or whatever you want to call it). Although it is normal and natural to feel grief when something tragic has happened in your own country or community, it is not our job to carry the world's grief and suffering in our hearts. There comes a point when we need to say 'enough' and disconnect if it benefits us to do so.

Personally, I do read the news (I prefer reading it to watching it). But when something dreadful happens such as a mass shooting or a war, I take a step back from the news and stop reading for several days. If I do not do this, I know that I will get sucked in to all the grief and drama, which is not good for my health.

When I am ready to go back to it, I skim the news with caution, and stay away from anything that is very sad or tragic.

Be Mindful of TV and Movies

Many empaths also cannot watch brutal, cruel or violent acts in TV shows and movies without being affected negatively.

As an empath, please don't feel that you 'should' become desensitized to such media. In my opinion, it is the times that we live in that are strange – not you!

Appendix B

Avoiding Negative Energies In Public Places

In this section, I wanted to include a couple of techniques that I often use when I find myself in a public place – either with a lot of people around (such as in the London Underground or in a crowded mall), or when I come across something that makes me feel sad when I am out and about.

The Bubble Technique for Shielding

As human beings, we consist of both a physical and an energetic body, which encompasses the chakra system, meridians, and the subtle bodies referred to earlier in this book.

Our energy field extends out from our physical body, and for many non-empaths (who have closed energy fields), it may only extend outward by an inch or two. For empaths, who have very large, open energy fields, the aura may extend much further from their physical bodies. When they find themselves in a crowded place (such as a mall or a sports stadium) where people are physically bumping or brushing up against them, this can cause some discomfort. That is because in this situation, people are not just touching the empath, or coming close physically, but are bumping up against this open energy field – and as a result, the empath can pick up on energies belonging to the people who are around them.

So empaths, when you are in a crowded space, you might like to use this bubble technique:

- Ask Archangel Michael to be with you
- Take 3 deep breaths
- Close your eyes, and visualise a big, blue, protective bubble being placed around the edges of your energy field. If your energy field extends out a long way, it will look like a large bubble. Also try to see it as a flexible bubble, that retracts and moves closer to your physical body when someone comes close to you.

This bubble is creating an energetic barrier between you and other people. So if someone brushes up against you in a crowded mall, their energy cannot reach you.

Blessings On Your Journey

Sometimes we come across sad or draining situations in life, or we pick up on challenging energies, and it is not something that we can do anything about in a concrete way.

An empath friend of mine has a technique that she uses when she comes across such scenarios, and I wanted to share it here in case it is helpful for someone else.

Next time you pick up on sad energies, or witness something upsetting, say inwardly (inside your mind) "Blessings on your journey - may you find healing," and then let it go. This does not mean we don't offer practical help to others, if we have some to give, but it does mean that when we can't help directly, we don't energetically carry the emotions around any longer than we need to.

Appendix C
Processing Grief

In Chapter Two, I talked about what I call the 'Emotional Projection Trap' – the idea that when we as empaths repress our feelings, we are more likely to pick up on (and be affected by) similar feelings in other people. In my experience, a primary reason for emotional empaths to pick up on other people's pain is because they have experienced a loss at some point that was not grieved or processed fully at the time.

Have you experienced a source of grief in your life that you did not acknowledge at the time? Here are some common experiences of loss:

- Death
- Breakup
- Betrayal
- Loss of a job or career
- Miscarriage
- Estrangement from family members or loved ones
- Loss of a beloved pet
- Trauma (which can trigger a sense of losing faith or losing safety)

- Retirement
- Loss of financial resources
- A child leaving home
- An accident or life-changing injury
- Loss of a dream or a personal goal

For some people grief can pile up, and go unaddressed for far too long. Often this happens when we find ourselves too busy, or too overwhelmed to feel what is really there.

Also, sometimes we don't even realize we are carrying grief; this is partly because it can be caused by something which "should" be a happy, positive event, such as emigrating and starting a new life in another country. We are encouraged to focus on the happier aspects of the change, but this can invalidate what we are really feeling, which is often a sense of loss for the things we left behind.

In this appendix section, you will find my thoughts on processing and releasing grief.

****

"The mourning process is not a matter of universal understanding - we cross the road when the widow walks by because we do not know what to say. We are embarrassed by her grief. We say, "Oh, she has taken it well" with admiration, meaning you can hardly tell she's just suffered a bit of a setback. We use these ridiculous expressions - "Draw a line under it." "Go on with your life." "Put it all behind you."

- Nigella Lawson (who lost her mother, sister and husband before the age of 40).

As the quote above illustrates, grief and sadness are not concepts our culture understands well or is comfortable with. Those who go through a loss are encouraged not to "dwell on it" or even process it properly, and as a result, some people carry around unresolved pain and grief in their energy fields.

What are some of the effects of not processing grief properly?

Unprocessed grief can cause:

- Depression
- Chronic pain
- Addictions/compulsive behaviours
- Chronic fatigue
- Overactive empathy

Time does not heal all wounds, and unprocessed grief does not necessarily go away - it can remind us of its presence in a variety of ways. It waits for the time when it will be recognised for what it is, and tended to appropriately. Sometimes it manifests somatically (in the body) in the form of physical pain or illness.

Here are some common signs and symptoms that you are carrying unprocessed grief or currently grieving:

- Intense sadness or yearning
- Crying
- Tiredness & exhaustion
- Irritability
- Gastrointestinal issues
- Preoccupation with loss; worrying that you are going to lose more people or good things in your life
- Nightmares
- Numbness and shock (especially in the first few months)
- Chest pain (especially where the heart is); a physical feeling of emptiness, a tightness in the chest
- Forgetfulness (short-term memory seems to disappear)
- Headaches or migraines
- Muscular pain
- Insomnia
- A feeling of restlessness or agitation
- Withdrawing from friends or social activities
- Anxiety/panic attacks
- Loss of appetite
- Eating too much
- Difficulties focusing/concentrating
- Difficulty making decisions

- Clumsiness (e.g. walking into furniture)
- A sense of guilt or thoughts of regret (sometimes over how the loss occurred)
- Anger – with God, yourself, the person who died, the whole world, or with the doctors who failed to save him/her
- Questioning your spiritual faith
- A lack of interest in things that used to give you joy

A Guide to Working Through Grief

Obviously every loss is different – not everyone grieves to the same extent, or in the same way. However, below are some of my hard-earned lessons on working through grief. I am sharing them here in case anyone finds them helpful:

- Do not try to defend yourself against grief. It will happen, and your job is to let it pass through you. Ride its waves. They will come and go, and each time they do, it will be slightly less intense than the last time.
- Other people will want you to defend yourself against it, because they do not want to see you suffer. It is not unusual for friends or loved ones who have not been through a bereavement or a loss to fail to understand what you are going through, and even to show a lack of support.
- The grieving process is different for each person. It is often helpful to read about other people's experiences, but keep in mind that your grief path may unfold differently.

- The aim is not to go back to how things used to be – a significant loss changes you forever.

- We do not ever completely finish the grieving process – sometimes a new grief will trigger an old one, and we need to go back and do a bit more grieving over that event, too. This does not mean that we are going to be constantly miserable as bad things happen. On the contrary, grieving is necessary to feel the positive emotions of life, too. If we do not let sadness pass through us, we can become numb.

- The first few months of a loss are sometimes the easiest, as shock can protect us from the full force of our grief. The understanding of the magnitude of what we have lost seeps into our consciousness bit by bit, but enough not to completely overwhelm us.

- Grief is experienced on multiple levels – not just emotionally, but also psychologically, spiritually and physically.

- A significant loss can take years to grieve. The first year is often the hardest, and the second year can be very difficult, too.

- Tears are important for processing grief. Some men may find it harder to cry than women (testosterone and social conditioning can inhibit tears). I often found that if I had not cried in a while, I would feel a lot of anger or irritability. I used to elicit tears by watching sad movies or listening to sad music, and this would be very cathartic, helping to ease the angry feelings. I made a playlist on YouTube of the saddest songs I could find. This practice is not wallowing – it is a healthy process of eliciting what may be repressed.

- You may also need to release anger. During my grief I took up boxing, threw crockery against the wall outside in the garden (that was an expensive habit), and I drove out to the middle of nowhere and screamed my lungs out. I also punched pillows.

- You may need to seek out new companions for this part of your journey. Online or offline support groups for people who are grieving can be helpful. You need to have someone around you who can validate or understand what you are going through.

- If you have lost someone to death, you might find it helpful to read books about the afterlife and mediumship – they can provide a source of comfort and inspiration.

- If you feel overwhelmed with grief, you might like to call on Archangel Azrael, who can help us with processing our heaviest emotions. Natalie Walstein, a student of my online courses, has this to say about her experiences working with this Archangel:

"I had a major health crisis last year and with it, my design business began fading away (which I had worked towards for the last several years)... I know now that this was all part of my path to becoming who I am now, but I had a lot of grief around it and especially all of the pressure around my family's reaction to it.

I eventually realized that I was grieving so much that it was affecting my ability to move forward. I had serendipitously heard about

Archangel Azrael and asked for him to help me deal with my issues and take my grief away. Less than two days later, I noticed that my grief had completely disappeared and I was ready to move forward and get on with whatever needed to be done. It has been one of my most powerful encounters working with angels!"

Appendix D

Further Reading for Overwhelmed Empaths

Trauma

- David Berceli, *Trauma Releasing Exercises (TRE): A Revolutionary New Method for Stress & Trauma Recovery* (BookSurge Publishing, 2005)
- Bessel Van Der Kolk, *The Body Keeps the Score: Brain, Mind, and Body in the Healing of Trauma* (Penguin Books, 2015)
- Peter Levine, *Waking the Tiger: Healing Trauma* (Atlantic Books, 1997)

Past Lives

- Roger Woolger, *Healing Your Past Lives: Exploring the Many Lives of the Soul* (Sounds True, 2010)
- Brian Weiss, *Many Lives, Many Masters: The True Story of a Prominent Psychiatrist, His Young Patient, and the Past-Life Therapy That Changed Both Their Lives* (Touchstone, 2012)

Grief & Loss

- Megan Devine, *It's OK That You're Not OK: Meeting Grief And Loss in a Culture That Doesn't Understand* (Sounds True, 2017)

- Catherine Sanders, *Surviving Grief ... and Learning to Live Again* (Wiley, 1992)
- Pat Schwiebert & Chuck Deklyen, *Tear Soup: A Recipe for Healing After Loss* (Grief Watch, 2005)

Boundaries

- Cheryl Richardson, *The Art of Extreme Self Care – Transform Your Life One Month at a Time* (Hay House, 2009)
- Anne Katherine, *Where to Draw the Line: How to Set Healthy Boundaries Every Day* (Touchstone, 2012)
- Melody Beattie, *Codependent No More – How To Stop Controlling Others & Start Caring For Yourself* (Hazelden Publishing, 2009)

The 'Emotional Projection Trap'

- John E. Sarno, *The Mindbody Prescription: Healing the Body, Healing the Pain* (Grand Central Publishing, 2001) - this book is about chronic pain so will not apply to all overwhelmed empaths, but I am including it here as I referred to his work in this book!

Being a Highly Sensitive Person

- Elaine N. Aron, *The Highly Sensitive Person: How to Thrive When the World Overwhelms You* (Broadway Books, 1997)
- Ted Zeff, *The Highly Sensitive Person's Survival Guide* (New Harbinger Publications, 2004)

Are you a Highly Sensitive Person in addition to being an empath?

The 'Highly Sensitive Person' is a term coined by psychologist Dr Elaine Aron. A highly sensitive person is someone who has a keener than average sense of hearing, vision, touch, taste and smell, and who is generally very sensitive to stimuli in their external environment.

In my experience working with empaths, many of them are also Highly Sensitive People (HSP's).

Here are some signs that you may be a HSP:

- You dislike loud noises like sirens, screaming babies and car alarms
- Noises that don't appear to bother other people (for example: noise from neighbours) really disturb you
- Smells that don't appear to bother other people affect you (e.g. someone wearing strong perfume)
- You need the lighting of a room to be 'just right,' and may have a dislike for bright or fluorescent lighting
- You feel stressed out when you're in a busy urban environment
- You are unusually sensitive to pain
- You pick up on subtle details in your environment that other people don't notice
- You are sensitive to caffeine
- You prefer peaceful, quiet environments to noisy, busy ones

- It is easy for you to feel overwhelmed when you have lots of different tasks to attend to
- You dislike high-pressure work environments
- You need a quiet place to withdraw to, and like to spend time alone
- You're easily moved emotionally by music, art, etc.
- You have food intolerances or sensitivities
- You fall in love quickly and feel overwhelmed by the feelings of ecstasy it causes, which can bring up anxiety

There are many lifestyle tips that are helpful for empaths & HSP's alike. I have not included any in this book because other authors have covered this topic extensively, and I have nothing new to add on the subject. You can find my book recommendations above, if you would like more information.

Appendix E

For Readers Who May Not Have Been Affected By Trauma

In Chapter Two, I covered several possible reasons why a person might become an empath. However, I did not cover every possible scenario that I have seen among my clients – including the one in which a person is simply born an empath. So in this section I am going to go into these a bit further, beginning with a question from a reader:

Hi Anna,

You talk a lot about the impact of early childhood traumas and relationship dynamics as the main factors in the development of empath gifts.

To be honest, I am not sure if these have affected me to the degree that other empaths may have been affected. The thing is, I am pretty sure I was born sensitive (my Myers-Briggs personality type is INFJ, which is a very sensitive type to begin with).

I did go through a couple of traumas and spent some of my childhood walking on eggshells, but I am pretty sure that I would have ended up sensitive, anyway. Besides, my brother went through the same traumas as I did, and did not end up a highly sensitive person or an empath. He has a totally different temperament from mine.

For this reason, I do wonder whether I would have ended up as an overwhelmed empath anyway, regardless of events in my early childhood?

~ Jade

****

Hi Jade,

I'm really glad you asked this question! In my work with empaths, I have observed that the majority of them (up to 80% as a rough estimate) have been affected by trauma. But I recognise that my client base may not fully reflect the general population of empaths out there!

Besides, I don't want to invalidate anyone who feels that the information does not apply to them – you know your life and your path better than anyone. So in this appendix I aim to put into perspective the role of the traumas and adverse relationship dynamics that I talked so much about in Chapter Two.

People Who Are Born With Empath Gifts

First of all, I too believe that we are born with our personalities already configured to some extent. (I am an INFJ as well).

Highly sensitive people like us are often born with empath gifts, which may or may not be latent. Sometimes they become activated because of the events that happen to us, and in other cases they may be fully activated from birth.

I believe that if a person comes out of the womb already an empath, then this circumstance is probably connected to that person's soul lessons.

Namely, this soul has decided that it wants to learn certain lessons during this lifetime, and being an empath will facilitate the learning of those lessons.

Empaths are clearly souls who have a great deal of compassion. In doing readings for empath clients, I have found that they are often learning to temper these positive qualities of theirs by adding some **boundaries** to the equation, so that they can be expressed in an effective way that benefits everyone concerned.

Let me give you a example of what this can look like in practice:

Angela is an empath who has a business as a healer. Her services are very much in demand, and she is a very compassionate person who cares deeply for her clients.

Angela has a strong desire to help everyone, and so she keeps her prices low – so low that she never seems to have enough money to get through the month. In addition, she sometimes does sessions for free, for people who can't afford them. She can't afford to take holidays either, and is always exhausted.

Over time, she gets burned out – and while Angela used to love her clients, she now begins to resent them a little bit (especially the ones who benefit from her free or discounted services). In the end, she decides that providing these services is just too draining for her, so she quits self-employment and gets a job. At least that way, she doesn't feel like everyone is draining the life out of her.

What is Angela missing in her work?

Boundaries.

She will not raise her prices or decline to give free or deeply discounted services, both of which might allow her to take holidays and stay well rested, so that she can give the best service possible to her clients.

Like Angela, many empaths explore these themes of **boundaries** or **the right balance between giving and receiving** in their lives.

So for those people who feel they have been empaths for as long as they can remember, and who do not resonate with the idea that their empath gifts may have been activated in their early years, this is one possible scenario.

Note that this situation can also apply to empaths who DO feel that the adverse events or relationship dynamics of their early years activated their empath gifts. I personally believe that this kind of trigger can occur by design, if the person has a soul contract to be an empath. So it is not an either/or scenario).

Past Lives

There is another reason a person might have their empath gifts activated from the outset.

It occurs when a soul has just come out of a stressful lifetime where they were not safe, and into a new incarnation, where they are safer – but they do not feel it, and as a result, the soul carries a past life complex on the issue of feeling physically threatened.

Here's an example of how such a past life scenario might manifest in a person's life:

Several years ago, I did a reading for a lady who sent a photo of her 4-year-old son, and asked me how many past lives had she had with him.

I saw that this child had come out of an incarnation in South America not that long ago. He had been a journalist in a country where journalists were considered a threat to the government, and as a result, the latter years of that lifetime were chaotic and frightening. He also lived in poverty, and thus that lifetime was all about survival.

Ultimately he was murdered by the ruling establishment, and the soul had come straight out of that horrid lifetime into this new one, with a stable, close-knit family in the U.S., loving parents, and enough food to eat. His soul no longer needed to be concerned with basic survival, as his physical and emotional needs were for the most part fulfilled.

However, the difference between these two lifetimes was like night and day, and the soul was having difficulty adjusting.

The mother confirmed that the child was noticeably more fearful and anxious than her other children. When she gave birth to him, she had the distinct impression that he wasn't very happy to be born.

How Past Life Complexes Trigger Empath Gifts

In Chapter Two, I explained the mechanisms by which present life trauma can activate a person's empath gift: when a child with a still-developing mind, body, and auric field goes through a trauma, he will usually expand his energy field beyond its usual borders, taking up more space energetically. And when this person has a very large auric field, he will be coming into contact with other people's energy fields on a regular basis, and this can mean that he is picking up on others' energies, too.

Beyond this, trauma can create tears in the etheric and other subtle bodies (especially if the trauma involved a sudden loss or separation). These tears affect the integrity of the energy field, rendering it more porous.

It is this combination of an **expanded, porous energy field** that characterises the empath child.

Past life complexes involving physical survival can have a similar effect on a young person, because children who do not feel safe or secure in their lives tend to develop larger auras and etheric bodies than children who do feel safe.

This is not something the child is going to do consciously or will be likely to understand – past life complexes exist out of sight and outside of our awareness, on the level of the unconscious mind.

So in conclusion, retaining a past life complex around feeling physically threatened can cause a child to expand his aura in just the same way as if he had been traumatised in his present life. This can be true even if he has had a very happy, uneventful childhood this time around.

If you suspect this may apply to you, the section in Chapter Two about past lives contains some recommendations and advice.

There is one more scenario that can affect the integrity of a child's etheric field and awaken his empath gifts:

Physical or Mental Illness

Physical or mental illnesses that we experience in our early years have the potential to weaken the etheric body, rendering it more porous. A child does not even have to be diagnosed with depression, anxiety or ADHD (to name a few common disorders that we see these days among children) to fall into this category. Sometimes a person in their formative years may experience sub-optimal levels of certain neurotransmitters which affect mood, and this can weaken the etheric body, contributing to the activation of empath gifts. However, this is rarely a trigger on its own, and is almost always experienced in conjunction with one of the other triggers.

As a side note, undergoing a general anaesthetic constitutes a major shock to the etheric body, and may also activate empath gifts.

If you are an overwhelmed empath who suspects that your empath gifts were originally activated or aggravated by poor physical/mental health, then treating and improving your health (whether through conventional medication or alternative means), may help to rein in your overactive empathy.

All of the above represent a number of possibilities for people who do not feel that their empath gifts were necessarily activated by traumas in their early years.

****

Let's go back to Jade's question – she also made reference to her brother, who underwent similar experiences but is not an empath. This is a good point, because there are many people in the world who suffer traumas, and yet only 8-10% of people in the world turn out to be empaths.

The fact is, not everyone responds to trauma in the same way.

Some people shut their hearts down in response to a trauma, and their energy fields become MORE closed off (rather than more open, like empaths' auric fields).

Keep an Open Mind

The scenarios given above may resonate with you as an empath more than the ones discussed in Chapter Two. However, I have worked with some empaths who have turned a blind eye to the traumatic events they have been through. Besides, when we undergo traumas before we form memories (prior to the age of 3), we are not as likely to remember them anyway!

So, if you identified as an overwhelmed empath at the beginning of this book, resonating with statements like:

- I often feel other people's experiences and emotions - experiencing them vividly and profoundly
- I am frequently unable to shake off other people's energies or emotions - these energies actually follow me around, even after the other person has moved on
- I have a hard time working out whether I am feeling my own energies and emotions, or someone else's
- I have become a hermit and withdrawn socially in order to avoid other people's energies
- I cannot visit crowded places such as shopping centres, stadiums, train stations, or nightclubs because the energies are so overwhelming

It is important to explore these concepts with an open mind. The more receptive you can be to the possibilities, the easier it is to identify and resolve your personal triggers, whatever they may be. The catalyst for your overactive empathy in the here-and-now could be just one factor, or it could be a combination of many.

Also note that the issues which commonly cause people to BECOME empaths are usually the same issues that aggravate empath gifts and cause them to go out of balance later on. So, for example, if you became an empath because you grew up with a parent who neglected your needs, the most significant personal trigger that may push you into empath overwhelm in adulthood is likely to be codependent relationships, where you are focusing more on the needs of other people, and less on your own.

About the Author

Anna Sayce is an Oxford-educated intuitive, healer, and teacher of spiritual development, who has worked with thousands of clients and students (many of whom are empaths) since 2007.

From childhood onward, Anna has been intensely curious and fascinated about what lies beneath the surface of life. And for two decades, she has been a keen student of topics such as intuition, past lives, healing, and the Akashic Records. She took what she learned through her own experiences and created a series of online courses, which aim to demystify the spirit world and make intuitive development practical, safe and easy.

Resources & Further Tools for Developing Your Empath Skills

- On my website I have a list of intuitive experiments, where you can use your empathic abilities to practice reading people in the public eye, using a photo of the person. You can also take a look at the results of the experiments and find out if you were accurate or not. Visit this page to have a go at those: AnnaSayce.com/Intuitive-Experiments-List

- Did you know that empaths have a real head start in developing their intuitive abilities in order to access spiritual guidance? If you are interested in developing your intuition, check out Anna's free e-course, which can help you with that. You can find it at: AnnaSayce.com/E-Course

Made in United States
Troutdale, OR
06/01/2024